From Seed To Salad

From Seed To Salad

A Step-By-Step Manual For Backyard Gardening

Frank Salerno

iUniverse, Inc.

New York Lincoln

From Seed To Salad
A Step-By-Step Manual For Backyard Gardening

iUniverse books may be ordered through booksellers or by contacting:

iUniverse
2021 Pine Lake Road, Suite 100
Lincoln, NE 68512
www.iuniverse.com
1-800-Authors (1-800-288-4677)

ISBN-13: 978-0-595-39322-0 (pbk)
ISBN-13: 978-0-595-83718-2 (ebk)
ISBN-10: 0-595-39322-5 (pbk)
ISBN-10: 0-595-83718-2 (ebk)

Printed in the United States of America

CONTENTS

ACKNOWLEDGMENT

I would like to express my deep gratitude to my daughter Annie, without whose unflagging help and computer wizardry, this book could not have been written.

A Word From The Author

When I moved into the home I currently live in there was a plot of land behind the house that appeared to have once served as a garden. It was sadly neglected and filled with weeds, and under the weeds, I was to find out later, was coarse sandy dirt, stones, pieces of coal, bits of construction debris, a broken bottle, and who knows what else. But as luck would have it, at the same time, a friend gave me a bunch of back-issue gardening magazines to read. The words inside struck me as magical—sun, soil, compost, seedlings, plants, vegetables—and they read like poetry. Until then I had never so much as grown a houseplant, but I did have recollections of my father having a garden in the back of our house when I was a boy. In fact, one of my recurring dreams to this day takes me repeatedly back to that place and time. I guess that it should have come as no surprise then that before long I was to be hooked on gardening. I had found my muse.

The first thing I did was to get rid of as much of that dirt as I could carry over to the local dump and replace it with as much leaf mold as I could bring back from the town composting facility, a place where the highway department piled up hundreds of truckloads of fallen leaves. It took a lot of heavy lifting and many trips back and forth, much of it with the help of my then-teenage children, but that's when, 30 years ago, I began my life as a backyard gardener, and I'm enjoying it as much now as I did then.

I've been retired for some time now, but I can still remember fondly the days when I'd come home after a hard day's work and step out after dinner to "play in the dirt." I'd pick up some pebbles, pull out some weeds, tie up some plants, and in general, simply take care of my little friends. I'd sit in a folding chair, soaking in the last of the sun for that day and triumphantly survey my surroundings. It might just as well have been a farm in the country, instead of this little piece of earth behind the house, but that's how much I enjoyed it. Picking the fruits of my labors was the icing on the cake.

I've learned a lot about gardening since those early days, and what I most learned is how little I knew back then. The things that went wrong and drove me to distraction then no longer do because I slowly learned that whenever there is a failure in the garden there is a reason for it, and those failures can be either corrected or prevented. Some things I learned I got from reading other people's writings, but many other things I learned through experimentation, trial and error, and all of it is in this book. There are little tricks here that I learned solely on my own and have never seen mentioned anywhere else.

The book makes no effort to cover the whole spectrum of edible plants. Instead, it focuses on only those plants that I found to be best suited for a small garden like mine, and in their popularity and their practicality. Thank you for sharing this book with me, and if you can have as much fun using it as I had putting it together, then we will both have won. Happy gardening.

Frank Salerno

1. From The Beginning

Picture this: You're in the throes of winter, at the end of February to be exact. You look out your window at the howling wind, the bare trees, and the frozen ground. Traces of snow and ice still remain from the last snowfall. The sun breaks through intermittently, but your mood is gray. Although officially the winter is only about 7 weeks old, it feels like it's been going on forever. Your mind drifts back toward summer with its blue skies, green lawns, foliage and flowers. How you miss those bright, warm days. They seem so far away.

But wait! You step over to the other side of the house where your home-built, plastic/polyethylene-covered window box is hanging, soaking in light, and where little green things are sprouting. These are your seeds, planted just a few weeks ago and now emerging—lettuce seeds, curly endives, onions, and leeks. You examine them closely, trying to gauge how much they've grown since yesterday. Oh, it must be at least a quarter inch! Suddenly, your mood is lifted. The heat and light that build up inside the box seem to radiate throughout the entire room and beyond. You look out the window again, at the hard, frozen ground, and this time in place of the lifeless earth, you see in your mind's eye the lush garden it was just a few months ago and will start to be again a few more weeks from now. You see big, fresh salads every night for dinner. You see luscious red tomatoes, tender green beans, and all that good stuff that comes out of the ground. Not so oddly, these delicate seedlings inside the window box, with their promise of things to come in the weeks and months ahead, make the winter feel a little less bitter, and they tell you that spring is right around the corner. Life feels good again.

This is the power that gardening has. Out of bare soil come little green things that become big green things that finally become a bounty of succulent vegetables. It's fun, relaxing and rewarding, but it can also be challenging and frustrating. At least, that is, until you get the hang of it, and that usually takes a while. If a line were to be formed by the number of would-be gardeners who quit in disappointment and despair every year because their early attempts fail so miserably, the line would be long indeed. But, that needn't happen. So long as we know the rules of do-and-don't, and follow them carefully, there's no reason why anyone can't grow a winning garden. Plants fail because gardeners make mistakes, they miss warning signs, or they neglect to give the plants the building blocks they need to thrive in the first place. This book hopes to put the fun and reward in gardening by learning from those failures and building on the successes.

2. Sun And Soil

The two most essential ingredients necessary for successful gardening are good sun and good soil. Without both, your efforts can only be marginally rewarded because plants will turn out to be stunted, weak, prone to disease and insect damage, and generally unproductive. With them, things will turn out magnificently better. Unfortunately, not every home gardener has the gift of a nice open field behind his house, blessed with naturally rich soil, and where he can get full sun straight through from sunrise to sunset. Even in the suburbs, where homes are spread out a bit more than they are in urban areas, most homeowners are boxed in between other houses and surrounded by shade trees, so full sunshine is at a premium. As a rule of thumb, plants need at least 6 hours of sun a day in order to grow well so the site chosen for your garden must have at least that minimum requirement. Anything less will compromise your results; anything more is a godsend. That makes a southern exposure for the garden the first imperative.

It has to be remembered that the sun moves across the sky, and the shadows it casts move along with it, although in the opposite direction. And so, as the day wears on it may first be that tree in your neighbor's front yard that throws the early-morning shadow onto your backyard, and then it may be the neighbor's house itself that throws off the noonday one. Or it might be that tall evergreen growing in your own side yard that casts the late-afternoon shadow. Consequently, unless you're one of those lucky few to have that open field I speak of, different parts of the garden catch the sun at different times of the day.

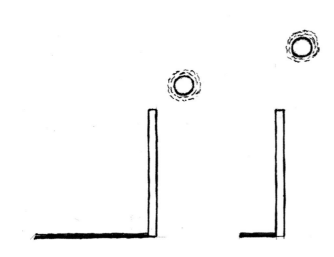

When planning your garden, this must be the first thing to be mindful of, understanding that as spring gives way to summer and the sun arcs higher and higher in the sky, the shadows will shift and change, gradually growing shorter in length and exposing more and more ground to the warming sun. (You can demonstrate this to yourself. In the latter part of winter, push a stick into the ground at the northernmost edge of a shadow, and then on successive days, at the same time each day, push more sticks into the ground. You will see how the shadow slowly creeps southward.) In June, on the first day of summer, the sun reaches its zenith and the shadows all but disappear. As we head toward the back-end of summer, the process reverses itself and the shadows start to move northward again. (The drawing on page 2 shows the differences in shadow lengths with the low winter sun and the high summer one.) All of this has to be reckoned with as you map out your garden and figure out how to get the most exposure that the sun has to offer for the entire growing season. We'll cover this in more depth later.

Incidentally…

The sun is 93 million miles away from the earth, and still it has the power and intensity to turn parts of our planet into death valleys and deserts. That's a lot of power. And yet, there are other parts of our planet that are essentially the same distance away and covered with permanent ice. How can it be?

It is the angle at which the sun's rays strike these different parts of the globe that makes the difference. The equatorial zone of the Earth receives the most direct rays of the sun all year round, and as a consequence, that's where the land can be unbearably hot. The two Polar Regions, on the other hand, receive only sharply angled, indirect rays, too weak to do much warming, making that part of the globe unbearably cold.

The Earth is tilted, and as it makes its yearlong journey around the sun, there comes a point when our northern hemisphere will reach its maximum angle toward the sun and receive its most direct rays. That's when summer arrives, along with its higher temperatures, longer days, and shorter shadows. And that's when the sun appears highest in the sky. Six months later, with the Earth having continued halfway around the sun, the northern hemisphere reaches its maximum tilt away from it. The sun's rays become more indirect; temperatures fall, and winter sets in. Meanwhile, the opposite is happening in the southern hemisphere so that when it's winter there, it's summer here, and vice versa.

3. Building Up The Soil

Having good soil is no less important than having good sun. It is here where our plants send out their root systems to draw in their nourishment and energy. It is here where that little seedling put into the ground in early spring gets to become that great big shrub of a plant loaded with deep-red tomatoes or fist-sized peppers. The gardening process begins and ends in the soil.

Good soil is loose in texture, dark in color, and holds moisture nicely. It feels velvety soft, and it even smells good. It's loaded with nutrients, the vitamins of the plant world. It also has a neutral pH factor. The ability of a plant to absorb nutrients is affected by the pH factor of the soil, which is a measure of the acidity of a soil, with zero representing extremely acidic and 14 representing extremely alkaline. It happens that most plants thrive best in the neutral range of 6.0 to 7.0.

One could say that it is in this narrow range where plants are happiest. If your soil is too much on the acidic side and you want to bring it closer to neutral, you can mix in some finely ground limestone. If it's too alkaline, adding ground sulfur will bring it back down. Most garden centers sell inexpensive kits that can test your soil's pH and make rough recommendations on how to amend it in order to bring it towards neutral. If you want more accuracy, you can take a sample of your soil to your local cooperative extension where for a small fee they will give you a thorough soil analysis and specific recommendations.

Good soil is not found; it has to be made. That is to say that if we dig a hole in virgin ground anywhere around our homes we will probably find a pile of poor-quality soil very similar to what was described in the beginning of this book. Trying to start a garden in such an environment would almost guarantee failure so we have to do something about it.

Of course, the easiest thing to do would be to call in a contractor or a landscaper who comes in with some heavy equipment, excavates the whole section that you've chosen for your garden, and then fills it in with some high-grade topsoil. But how much fun is that? Instead, you can undertake a modified version of the same thing yourself.

All plant life is composed of organic matter, and when that life breaks down and decays through microbial action, it returns to its basic mineral elements, ready to be recycled into new plant life. Soil that's rich in organic matter is rich in the lifeblood of plant life.

Building up your soil can start with burying all the plant material you can get your hands on. Table vegetable scraps are good, and of course you can include them in your soil-building program, but there's a limit to how many of them you can collect. Grass clippings are good if free of weed killer and if not put down in heavy layers that will bind into thick mats, taking too long to decompose. Best of all, because they are so abundantly available, and because they break down so readily, are tree leaves. In the fall you can have access to all the leaves you can carry. If you run out of your own leaves you can use your neighbor's leaves or even drive around town and pick up somebody else's leaves, all bagged and ready to go. Avoid oak leaves and pine needles because they are acidic.

At the end of the gardening season, and as each section of your garden is done being picked, pull out the plants and start digging a large pit in the middle of that section as far down as you can go before you hit bottom, that sub-layer of earth that is lifeless, hard-packed and has the virtual consistency of cement. You can't know how deep that will be until you start digging, but try to get down at least 12 inches. Pile the dug-up soil alongside two sides of the pit, removing any stones and debris you find along the way, and then throw in the plants, chopped up with the point of a shovel, and your collection of leaves. Don't fill the hole up all at once, but rather, throw in a layer of plant material, followed by a layer of soil, leaves again and so on until the hole is finally capped with soil. On top of each combined layer, sprinkle in a handful of lime and toss in a bucket of water. The lime will help sweeten the soil, and the water will help start the decaying process. Move on to the next hole, then the next section, until the whole garden has been covered.

The chemical breakdown will start almost immediately and continue throughout the winter, but it will move slowly, depending on how mild or severe the winter turns out to be. Those parts of the garden that get some winter sun will fare better than those parts that are in perpetual shade, but that's of no concern because the real breakdown doesn't start in earnest until the ground warms up the following spring and summer. In the meantime, rain and melting snow will seep down into the mix keeping it moist and active.

By the time the next season ends, when it's time to repeat the soil renewal process and you dig your first hole, you will find that while you weren't looking all that plant material that was buried underground ten months before has disappeared almost without a trace, and in its place are ribbons and layers of dark brown humus. The breakdown is now complete. By repeating this process year after year you will end up, over time, with a garden full of rich, chocolate-colored soil.

- Save some of this dark soil. Screen it to remove stones and pebbles, throw in a couple handfuls of vermiculite or perlite, mineral soil amendments available at your garden center, that help to keep the soil loose, a small handful of 5–10–5 fertilizers, and a handful of lime. Mix it thoroughly and store a couple bucketsful indoors. You will use it for next spring's seedlings.

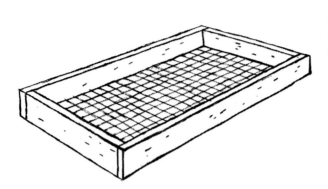

Left: The soil screener is 24 by 36 inches, made with 1-by-6-inch board. The bottom is covered with ¼-inch hardware cloth, nailed in place using screen molding.

Incidentally…

Nature planned it well: For life to continue, one generation must lead to another generation which must lead to still another, and on and on. In the plant world, this is accomplished through seed production. Trees do it, flowers do it, and vegetables, too, do it.

It would be nice to believe otherwise, but that apple that we pick from a tree was not put there for our pleasure and consumption; it was put there so that in the natural world, unmolested by humans, the apple would fall from the tree in the autumn, its flesh would rot away, and the following spring, at least some of its seeds would take root and become other apple trees. In that way, apple trees would be assured a permanent place on Earth. The fact that man came along at one point in the evolutionary chain and discovered that apples taste good, is a very happy convenience for him.

And that's what is happening in our backyards. The aim of all the plants in our garden is to form seeds. In some cases, the vegetables we pick and eat *are* the seeds, inside their also-edible pods—peas and beans. With tomatoes and peppers, it's the pods that we desire, and they happen to have seeds inside. Had all these things been growing in the wild, and left unpicked, they would do what nature designed them to do, fall to the ground, and take root.

The leafy plants we eat, and the root crops—the lettuces, spinaches, beets and radishes—if left to reach the ends of their life spans, would all eventually grow seed heads, and some of them can be downright flowery. Onions and leeks are notable examples, forming beautiful tennis-ball sized, pastel flower heads. The broccolis are in their own class; we eat the flower heads before they actually flower, and they, too, would eventually turn to seed.

4. Container Gardening

Containers can stretch the available space you have for gardening. They can be lined up around a patio, against a wall or fence, or placed anywhere else where it would be impractical or inconvenient to grow plants in the ground. If you are in a situation where sunlight is really minimal and the will is strong enough, containers can be moved around to follow the sun. The bigger the container is, the better. At the very least, you can start with the 5-gallon plastic buckets that carry potato salads and cold slaws to your local deli. Maybe you have a friendly counterman who would save you a few. Spackle containers, if you're willing to put in the effort to clean them, are good as well. And how about those big buckets that carry pool chemicals? You could even consider some reasonably priced plastic storage containers. Whatever you settle on, make sure to drill some ¼-inch holes in the bottoms for drainage.

Not all plants are suitable for container gardening, especially if the containers are on the small side. You might have some little success with a "patio tomato," perhaps, but not with full size tomatoes. You can no doubt grow a cabbage, but it will not be the cabbage you are hoping for. Even a lettuce plant will grow half the size in a container than it will in the ground. Peppers do well, one plant per pot; peas and beans do well, several plants per pot; and turnips, one or two per container do well, as do herbs. Remember, though, that in every case, plants and their fruits grow much bigger in the ground, but containers are still a great way to supplement the garden.

Incidentally…

In this age of technological advances that reach us at breakneck speed, changing the way we live almost moment to moment, offering us newer, better, bigger, smaller, cheaper, and more expensive products and gadgets even before the warranties on our recently acquired ones expire, isn't it comforting to know that in our gardens we are still growing tomatoes the same way our ancestors and their ancestors did, and that somewhere in China or India there are cottage farmers still doing the same thing? Notwithstanding the fact that all over America, many family farms have sold out to agribusinesses or developers, in our backyard gardens we can almost feel like time has stood still. We are still using the basic tools and techniques to grow tomatoes that were used generations, and even centuries ago. Don't you just love it?

---

5. COMPOSTING

Containers have to be filled with soil so here's where composting comes into play. The principle of composting is the same as that of building up the soil except that it's done above ground instead of below. Again, the goal is to turn plant material into nutrient-rich soil. By picking a spot in an unused corner of the garden, where you can throw all the scrap material that comes out of the garden—surplus seedlings, root balls, depleted plants, etc.—and adding in an occasional shovel full of soil, you can form a little compost pile. Inside the pile, the plant material will slowly break down. Turning the pile over periodically with a garden fork, top to bottom and bottom to top, to keep it fresh and airy, and by continually adding to it and keeping it moist, you can accumulate a supply of nutrient-rich material that can be used as a side dressing mixed into the soil around your growing plants, to pot new seedlings, or to re-pot established plants.

To fill the containers you will need to step up the composting regimen. After the gardening season is over and you've finished the pit-filling process, pick a spot where you will get the most sun that's available through the winter months, and start above ground the same process you've just completed below ground, piling layer upon layer of leaves and soil, a little lime and lots of water, into a high mound. The higher the mound, the more compost you will have available when you need it. When done, level out the top of the mound and create a saucer-like impression in it to catch the rain or snow that falls in the coming months. And now the fun can begin.

Allow several weeks or so for the mound to settle and the degradation to begin, and then go out whenever the weather is mild and you're feeling outdoorsy, and turn the pile around with a garden fork. There will be days throughout the winter when the pile will be frozen and can't be worked, and days when it will have thawed, but as the season wears on you will be surprised to see how many pleasant days there are, even in January and February, that will allow you to do this. Each time you toss the pile you will be breaking up the clumps of leaves that stick together, and you will be airing it out. As the weeks roll by, and you feel yourself getting closer and closer to spring, you will also be surprised to see the leaves seemingly disappearing before your very eyes. By the time March arrives you will have enjoyed some outdoor winter exercise, and the pile will have turned into a crumbly mass of dark soil and fragmented leaves, just right for filling the containers. (Not even a walk along the beach on a mild winter day can be as much fun as that.)

- When you empty the containers in the fall, throw the plants in the pits and the root balls on the compost pile, and scrape out the sides of the containers so they can be stacked together and stored indoors for the winter. Most plastics don't weather well if you leave them out in the cold.

- If your budget allows, a leaf shredder will greatly reduce the leaf volume and make them quicker to break down both in the compost pile and in the ground.

6. Raised Beds

As you can imagine, if you put more material into the ground each year than comes out of it, the level of the soil is going to gradually rise. This gives you a good reason to establish some raised beds. A raised bed is a garden plot that is higher than the natural ground level around it. By building a short wall around the plot, say 6 or 8 inches high, and then filling it in, you will be giving your plant roots a lot more room to grow in, and the plants will love that. This is particularly true where the native soil is of especially poor quality, making it easier to build it up than build it down. Raised beds also make it easier to pick low-lying crops such as lettuce, radishes, etc., by bringing them up closer to your reach.

The amount of garden space you have to work with, and the amount of effort you're willing to invest in it, will determine what materials to use to build the walls around the beds. Pressure-treated wood would normally be a great choice because of its durability, but the toxins in the wood will leach into the garden soil, and that's not good for the plants. Plain wood planks or beams can be used, but they will rot quickly, necessitating replacement too often. Cinder blocks are a good choice if you have the space to spare. They're heavy, and they're sturdy, but they are also bulky, and they take up a lot of room. Patio paving stones are ideal. They're only a few inches thick, and sticking them in the ground halfway, either horizontally or vertically, and running them edge-to-edge around the perimeter of the plot, will establish the wall. The pressure exerted against the

walls as the plot fills up with soil will have a tendency to push the stones outward, requiring periodic readjustment, but if you're willing to go that extra mile and cement them together you could build a much more stable wall, requiring very little maintenance. The drawing at left shows a raised bed.

7. Constructing An Incubator And Cold Frame

Growing your own seedlings indoors as opposed to buying them at the garden center has many advantages, not the least of which is the cost savings. Another bonus is that when you grow your own seedlings you will always end up with more than you would ordinarily buy, something you will come to appreciate later on. Growing your own will also ensure you a better quality product and allow you to precisely time your planting schedule.

At the garden centers, the best plants and seedlings are found during the very first days of planting time when the whole town seems to descend in droves. Soon after, the good ones are gone, and only the poorest plants are left. Later in the season, if you want to do a second crop, the centers will be cleaned out and there won't be a plant to be found. Last but not least is the great satisfaction you will feel taking the gardening experience from the very beginning to the end. However, whether you can or cannot grow your own seedlings depends on certain conditions.

The first thing you will need is a sunny window, a south-facing one because in our northern hemisphere that's the side of the house that gets most of the sun. Then you will need a window box, a plant incubator if you will, to hang outside that window, a window and a box both large enough to hold several trays of seedlings.

Let's take a moment here to review the absolute necessity of sunlight in gardening and why an incubator can be so important: Anyone who has ever tried to grow a potted plant on a sunny windowsill knows how hard it is to get a robust plant. As it is growing, a plant reaches toward the sun, or in the absence of sun, it reaches toward the light. A windowsill gets only frontal light. A growing plant needs more than that, and when the sun is insufficient, the plant is forced to reach harder and farther for that essential light. So, paradoxically, although a young plant with insufficient sun may appear to be growing rapidly, it will be doing so only because it is reaching so hard, becoming a spindly imitation of what it wants to be.

Seedlings need all the sunlight they can get, and from every direction, if they are to grow into sturdy plants. They need sunlight coming at them from the left, the front, the right and the top. A box, wrapped in clear plastic and jutting far out of the window, fills the bill exactly. A south-facing incubator will catch the rising sun, the setting sun, and most importantly, the overhead daytime sun, and that's what seedlings love, to be bathed in sun.

Building an incubator will require some carpentry skills and some custom designing because dimensions and construction will depend on the size and nature of your window. The incubator you find in the back of the book is identical to one that I've been using for years, and it can accommodate three standard 10-by-20-inch cell pack trays with a little room to spare for several seeding cups. Unless you are lucky enough to have a window the same size as mine, that incubator can serve as a template only. If you the reader, or an associate, have the skills required it should be a piece of cake. Otherwise, a local carpenter can probably be found to help you out.

And what if you don't have that big, sunny window in which to put an incubator? Can you still grow your own seedlings? Well, yes, in a cold frame.

A cold frame is similar to the incubator in that it too is a plastic covered box, this time with a removable top, used to protect plants against the cold. Whereas the incubator sits in the window, with the indoor air to back it up, the cold frame sits outside, with only the heat captured inside it to protect the plants.

As the seedlings grow in size and fill up the incubator they've got to make way for new seedlings so the next stop for them is in the cold frame. The cold frame is a miniature greenhouse where plants start to get a taste of the outdoors in preparation for being set into the ground. Its design, also illustrated in the back of the book, is built around standard cell pack trays and can be followed exactly.

If you can't have an incubator, you can raise your seedlings in the cold frame, but on a different time schedule than you would use with the incubator. Because it can still get pretty cold inside the cold frame on overcast days, mid-March is about the earliest recommended time for putting incubator-started plants there, even the cool-weather kind. Trying to start seedlings there at that time would be chancy at best. This means that you will have to move the planting schedule shown in chapter 12 ahead by at least 3 weeks, starting onions, say, on March 1 instead of February 7, and lettuce, say, on March 14 instead of February 21, and so on. Once you get to April, when 50-degree days become more commonplace, and cold frame-grown seedlings will have a better shot, you can switch back to the original schedule, but you may have lost that early jump-start that makes incubator-grown plants so special, and second crops a guarantee.

8. To Grow Or Not To Grow

Looking at a seed catalogue makes one feel like a kid in a candy store. I want this! I want that! I want this, and that too. Sure, everyone would like to grow tomatoes and berries and herbs and watermelons and everything else that looks so lush and delicious in the catalogue, but unless you have one of those big open fields in full sun that we spoke of earlier, it's not going to happen. Nor will it happen if you crowd everything your heart desires into the limited confines you have to work with. Healthy plants need room to grow. Huddled up together, they not only become cluttered and grungy, but they also become havens for destructive insects.

With so many vegetables to choose from, and so little room to grow them, deciding on what to plant can be daunting, but studying their growth patterns can help. Melons and squash are vine crops. They creep and crawl along the ground gobbling up great big pieces of turf so unless you have the space they need you might have to take a pass on them. Tomatoes are vine crops, too, but they are far less aggressive, and they can be trained to grow up a pole rather than along the ground so needless to say, tomatoes go into the seed basket. Peas, even the bush kind, grow on vines that tend to grow higher than the seed packets allege, but the plants and the fruits are lightweight and can be trained to grow on a trellis.

A trellis needn't be a grand store-bought affair made of wood or plastic latticework and used to train roses and vines. It can be mimicked by driving several stout poles into the ground 4 feet apart—the number depending on how big a span you want to cross—and running nylon string across the poles in 6 inch increments. More string, strung vertically every 6 or 8 inches, and knotted around the horizontal strands, will form a grid pattern, much like a fisherman's net. As the peas grow you can weave them through, and up along, the net. Against a south-facing wall is ideal.

Above: Sugar Snap peas several weeks apart and growing out of 5-gallon containers while climbing a string trellis set up against a wall. After this photo was taken, vertical strings were added to the horizontal ones to reduce sagging.

Cucumbers, another member of the vine family, can also be had in the so-called bush variety, but even they tend to get carried away, necessitating tying them up against a trellis or along a fence. The thing about cucumbers, though, is that after many weeks spent cultivating them, they reach the picking stage at the same time that lettuce is growing abundantly and you will soon be crossing over to tomatoes, making them seem, some might say, redundant. When I grow them, I give them low priority and grow them in containers up against a fence and out of the main garden.

Bush bean seed packets also make claims to grow on short bushes, but they too have the tendency to vine out about 4 feet or so. However, they can be managed by planting them against a trellis, or in a rectangular plot with stout stakes driven into the ground at the four corners of the plot and then boxing the beans in by wrapping string tightly around the stakes as the beans grow upward and outward. Their seeds go in the basket.

Lettuce plants are no-brainers. They are easy to grow and come in varieties that you will never see in your local market. Root crops, such as radishes, beets and turnips are also easy to take. They use up little room, grow rather quickly, and after being picked they allow you to grow a second crop of either themselves or something else. Peppers, broccoli, and Swiss chard don't grow in rows like the root crops do, but stand on their own. They require minimal maintenance, and it's easy to give them a yes.

Onions are one of the easiest things to grow, with one of the biggest payoffs—after harvesting they can be kept in a cool garage and used into early spring before they begin to sprout and turn soft. Yellow Globe onions are good keepers, but they also come in many other varieties. Leeks, a close relative, can be grown alongside the onions but with this one difference: They are planted in a trench a foot deep, and 6 inches wide, and as they grow, the trench is gradually filled in with compost, soil or any form of plant debris. It is that part of the leek that grows underground that yields the white stalk that makes leeks the treat that they are. Place the trench in a spot that you can access easily. You may have to prop up the sides of the trench with scrap wood or heavy cardboard supported by wooden pegs to keep the sides from caving in. As the trench fills up, you can pull out the supports. Both onions and leeks leave room for a succession crop.

What you won't find in our backyard garden is spinach because it has a short growing span, petering out in the summer's heat. In its place we have Swiss chard, a practical substitute that thrives throughout the entire season producing a steady flow of tennis racquet-sized leaves that keep replacing themselves as they are cut off. Three plants, or even two, can deliver a small family a steady supply of greens. Nor will you find egg-plants. They are fun to grow because of their size and striking color, but they are very care-intensive. The plants grow large and the fruits heavy, requiring a great deal of staking and tying, but that is a small complaint compared to the fact that they are extremely insect prone, too often requiring too many sprayings to keep the maggots away. (At least, that has been the case for me.) Furthermore, they are one homegrown vegetable that shows little or no superiority to store-bought varieties anyway so I sadly take a pass on them.

Regrettably, the ever-popular corn doesn't make the cut either, but for a very different reason. Corn needs to be planted in multiple rows to cross-pollinate for it to succeed so if you don't have a big enough garden you won't have the room for it. Of course, all gardeners will eventually find their own rhythms and develop their own wish lists of things to grow. Trial and error is the teacher.

In the back of the book you will find two garden layouts that I've settled on after years of experimentation, one for odd years and one for even years, in order to follow some form of crop rotation. These are very personalized designs that can only serve as rough models to give you some ideas. The minimum spacing that I allow between the main plants is 24 inches, and often more. If you are a beginning gardener your soil may not be ready to deliver the plants that will fill those spaces, but in time it will.

Incidentally…

During the course of my work, when I made service calls to people's homes, I came across lots of clients who had backyard gardens, or reasonable facsimiles of such, who were more than willing to show them off to me. I was often amazed by what I saw, and as I reflect back now, years later, I keep wondering if my mind was playing tricks on me.

One fellow had a couple of broccoli plants growing in a tiny piece of dirt surrounded by lots of cement that was part of a 6-house common driveway, leading to all of the individual garages. The plants were riddled with cabbage moth holes, and he seemed completely oblivious to the fact, while waiting for his broccoli to grow. One woman had a bunch of tomato seedlings growing in a large cluster, all the plants two and three inches apart. She had scattered some seed in the ground, and was now waiting for the plants to grow and the tomatoes to follow. She thought that that was how it was done. One fellow had his plants lined in a row on a concrete slab, growing in coffee cans. If I hadn't seen these things with my own eyes, I wouldn't have believed them.

9. Inter-Planting And Succession-Planting

Some vegetables, lettuce being a prime example, grow relatively fast and are pulled out of the ground whole. This is in contrast to other plants, like tomatoes and peppers, which need the entire season to reach maturity and are continually being picked. Filling your garden with lettuce where the long-term plants will go later allows you to pick a steady supply of salad greens while the others are slowly taking over. Other fast-growing plants, like those of the broccoli family, beans, peas, and beets allow you to squeeze out a succession crop, potentially giving you a freezer full of veggies for the winter.

Using our model garden as a guide, sketch out your garden layout on a sheet of graph paper, including all measurements. Decide what you'd like to grow, and draw up a plan marking the exact locations of each of your choices. Allow for ample spacing between plants, and don't forget to include the containers in your planning. Keep in mind everything you've learned earlier about sun and shade, and plan accordingly. That section of the garden that gets the most sun should get planted first. The section that may be in shade until the sun moves higher should be planted last. Ideally, tall plants are located in the back so as not to shade the shorter ones in the front. In a small garden that is not always realistic, but it's a good rule to follow as far as one can. It may take you a couple years to figure this all out, but you will. When it becomes time to transfer your sketch over to the actual garden, place sticks into the ground at all the main planting locations so you can leave those spots free for later.

- We don't show leeks in the sketches of our model gardens because we don't grow them every year. When we do, we borrow a 12-inch strip from the onion patch.

10. ROTATING YOUR CROPS

Crop rotation is a farming practice that calls for switching plant locations from year to year. It's done to allow plants to leave behind any disease or insect problems they may have suffered the previous year. As you will see when you get to chapter 21, where we deal with the subject in depth, insects are a constant concern in the garden. In most cases, insects tend to gravitate to favored plants, and then presumably bury themselves and over-winter in those same locations. So then, theoretically at least, by changing plant locations every year we can leave those insects and any diseases behind. In a small garden, where plots are separated by no more than a few feet, it becomes more a case of being "better safe than sorry."

More important to the rotation process, however, is the fact that each species of plant draws from the soil its own set of mineral requirements, and by changing locations we allow the plants to tap into "new soil." In its truest form, farmers will often leave large sections of their farms to lie fallow for a year or two in order to give the land a chance to recharge. We can't go that far, but we can at least give our plants the benefit of the doubt by moving them around a bit. We do that with our model garden when we lay out our two plans, labeled "Odd Years" and "Even Years."

Incidentally...

My wife and I are empty nesters now, and although a good portion of what comes out of my garden goes to friends, neighbors, and our children, when they happen to come by, the bulk of it goes into the freezer so that we can enjoy it throughout the year. Stuffed peppers are our favorite, but we also put away broccoli, beans, peas, Swiss chard—everything that I grow. Not only does it all come in handy, but also there's no telling how much we save in food bills.

Before this, though, when the kids were high school age and thereabouts, "Veggie Night" was a big deal. That's when for dinner we had nothing but vegetables from the garden: beet salad, made with sliced beets and onions, oil, vinegar, and oregano flakes; broccoli, sautéed in olive oil and garlic, with some soy sauce added; broccoli raab sautéed in oil, lots of garlic, with some hot pepper flakes added, and a bit of water to make it juicy; sugar snap peas with butter; green beans, either with butter or sautéed with onions and soy sauce; and of course the piece de resistance: the big tomato salad, made with olive oil, sliced fresh peppers, oregano, lots of garlic, and lots of fresh basil. It was to die for. Even today, my contribution to any summer barbecue that I'm invited to will be the big tomato salad.

---

11. STARTING YOUR SEEDLINGS

So far all of our attention has been paid to preparing ourselves for the main event, and it's time now to start growing some seedlings. After all, that's why we're here. To get the most from your garden, timing is essential. As the winter drags on and we begin to have visions of tomatoes and green beans dance in our heads, the wish to get started becomes irresistible, especially when we experience those first balmy days in February and March that have that tantalizing feel of spring. However, balmy days notwithstanding, we are still far away from putting anything into the ground, but until then there's a lot that we need to do.

In the garden world there are cool-weather crops and warm-weather crops. The cool-weather kind goes into the garden first because, as the brand implies, they are more tolerant of cool conditions. Among these, to name just a few, you will find lettuce, peas, broccoli and radishes—all the things we start early in the season. Warm-weather crops are more sensitive to the cold, and they get planted later when things warm up. These include tomatoes, peppers, beans, and eggplants if you choose to grow them.

Under the best conditions most seeds will germinate in 2 to 4 days, and some will take a little longer, the differences usually depending on several controllable factors. Sometimes you can keep seeds lying around for two, three, and even four years and still have them work for you, but they tend to become more unreliable with each passing year. Fresh seeds, on the other hand, dated for the current year, will generally activate much quicker than held-over seeds.

It's an intriguing idea to save seeds from your own garden, thinking that the seeds from that great big tomato you just picked will generate more great big tomatoes just like it, but it doesn't quite work out that way. Seeds that you buy are most often hybrids, carefully developed by professional seed growers by interbreeding plants with special qualities. When the seeds from the hybrid plants grow into the next generation, the resultant seeds from their fruits will genetically begin to drift back to their former histories and start losing the qualities that they were originally bred for. For example, the first-generation seeds from a tomato that was bred for cold hardiness will already have started to lose some of that hardiness, and with each succeeding generation more of that quality is lost.

Seeds and their seedlings like warm more than cool so a proper spot must be found for them to germinate. Starting them atop the refrigerator, where heat from the motors tends to accumulate, can be an option. A better spot, though, would be atop the boiler in the furnace room, usually the warmest spot in the house.

Seeds also like a gentle place in which to start life. Seed starter is a soil-less commercial mixture of a light, fluffy, sterilized combination of peat moss, perlite or vermiculite, and nutrients. It encourages seeds to sprout more quickly and with greater reliability than they would in ordinary soil. Give them that, and some bottom heat, and your seeds will have a great head start.

Generally speaking, seedlings need 6–8 weeks between sprouting and planting so we are always planning that far ahead. On Feb. 21 you can start planting some lettuce seed, some curly endive, and dwarf marigolds. Small plastic containers or cups, such as those that carry yogurt, margarine, and other dairy products, are ideal for starting seeds. Drill a few small holes in the bottoms of the cups for drainage, fill them nearly to the top with wet seeding mixture (not too wet), spread on some seeds, and top them off with ¼ inch more mixture. This depth is about right for most seeds, but check the backs of the seed envelopes to be sure.

Don't be overly generous with the number of lettuce and endive seeds you spread because you don't want all of your salad plants growing at the same rate. When you start picking them you will want them to mature in a sequential order rather than all at once so it's wiser to plant fewer seeds now and more later to give yourself a steadier flow. Seeds like those of the tomato and pepper are easy to count out because they are relatively large, but those like lettuce and endive are too small to separate, which makes it hard to keep count, but generally speaking having a couple dozen of them always growing at different stages would be about right

With the seeding done, wet the mixture down a bit more with a spray bottle and either put the covers back on the cups to keep them from drying out, or seal them in a plastic bag, Place them in a warm, fuzzy spot, and then keep an eye on them. Don't forget to label the cups so you can remember what's in them and the date they were planted.

At this stage, your incubator should be almost ready to be placed in the window because things are about to move quickly. The moment the first seeds sprout they are reaching for light. Most seeds sprout during the night. This is true whether it's happening naturally outdoors or under simulated conditions indoors. You should check the cups every morning, and at the very first signs of life those cups must go into the incubator, first one, then the next, and then the next. Your timing is important because if a sprouting cup is left to sit in the dark for even a half-day or more, you'll end up with long, thread-thin little creatures unable to hold themselves up, and you'll have to start over.

In the incubator you should keep the cups moist, but not wet, until the second set of leaves, called the "true" leaves, are formed. At this stage the seedlings are ready to be moved out of their common container and into individual cells. Gardening centers sell cell packs in a wide assortment of combinations and sizes, but a good starting point can be the four-cell units, each cell about 2 inches square, which can fit into a tray holding 12 units. That would amount to 48 seedlings in a tray.

To fill the cell packs you can refer back to chapter 3 on building up the soil. You will recall that we put aside some garden soil to save for another day. This is that day. Wet the soil slightly and use it to loosely fill the cell packs. (If you didn't put soil aside, you can continue using seeding mixture for this next step.) Tap the seedlings out of their cup, root ball and all. Drop the root ball down on a sheet of newspaper several times from 6 inches high. This will help to loosen up the ball. Using a sharpened stick (coffee stirrer), gently separate the roots while lightly pulling the seedlings apart, holding them by their first, unessential leaves. Poke a hole in each cell with your finger, set the seedling in, a bit lower than it had been in the cup, press the soil down and around the seedling and, using a spoon and soil, top off the cell and press the soil in again lightly but firmly. To prevent plant shock when done, do not place the transplanted seedlings in direct sunlight. Instead, water them gently, and place the tray aside for a couple hours before putting it in the incubator.

Since you earlier had drawn up a careful garden layout, you should know exactly how many plants of each variety you will need. Grow some extras. If you are planning on five tomato plants, for example, grow eight. If it's two broccolis, grow four. Think in terms of multiples of four because that's how many plants you can grow in each 4-cell pack. You should always be prepared for unexpected circumstances so having extras in reserve makes sense. It's hard to guess how many lettuce plants you will need so just grow them by the tray full.

Set the plants in the incubator in the morning and take them in at night. Those cups that are still in their early germinating stages are best returned to their warm and fuzzy spot so that they can continue to sprout. Plants that are more advanced can be left on the floor or kitchen table—anywhere so long as it is indoors. Having everything in trays will facilitate the movements back and forth. In the morning it's best to wait until the sun is up high enough to have warmed the inside of the incubator before moving the trays back in. On sunless days, allow the heat of the room to mix with the air inside the incubator first.

Try to have a gallon-or-two of rainwater or melted snow in the house at this time, and use it exclusively in the incubator. Use a watering can with a small spout opening that will deliver the water slowly so as not to disturb the soil too much.

- Allow a cup to dry out a day or two before transplanting into the cell packs. A drier root ball falls apart more easily than a wet one, making the seedlings easier to separate. If the ball is wet, and hard to tease apart, let it sit on newspaper awhile so it can dry out somewhat.

- Not all seeds germinate at the same rate. In the same container, some may sprout several days apart, meaning that when it's time to separate them, some will be more immature than others, requiring extra delicacy in handling them.

- When plants are about 4 weeks old you can start giving them some weak liquid fertilizer every 7 to 10 days.

- As the sun gets higher it also gets hotter, and the plants will need watering more often, maybe several times a day. If you're leaving the house for any length of time, even for a couple hours on a very bright day, you must either shade the plants with newspaper or cardboard or take them out of the sun entirely until you return. Those small cell packs have very little moisture reserve, and they can very quickly dry out.

- Plants are amazingly resilient. If they inadvertently do dry out and begin to droop, they will quickly recover after watering, especially if they are taken out of the sun until they revive. But once the leaves appear scorched it may be too late.

- Over-watering can be as damaging to plants as under-watering. Allow at least the surface of the seedling containers to dry out a bit before giving them more to drink.

Onions and leeks are two of the hardiest edible plants around, able to withstand some pretty harsh weather. (Notice how wild onions are usually the first things that pop out of the lawn during the winter.) They can go into the garden in early April when little else can survive and, allowing for the 6-to-8-week growth window the seedlings will need, between sprouting and planting, you can start their seeds on Feb. 7. Both plants have long roots so you should sow them in tall containers, 8 to10 inches high. If your aim is to grow just a couple dozen onions and/or leeks, a tall cottage cheese or ricotta container will do. If you would like to grow more than that you will need wider containers, 8 inches across.

Use the garden soil to fill up most of the container, and top it off with a couple inches of seeding mixture. Using garden soil to fill the bulk of the containers is an economy move and more. Onions and leeks bypass the cell pack stage, going straight from their common container into the ground so they will be growing in the same medium for almost 8 weeks. The soil is loaded with sustainable nutrients while the seeding mixture has only a limited supply.

You can be fairly liberal with onion seeds because they grow like grass and can tolerate some crowding so spreading a half-packet of seed between two wide containers will give you a healthy supply of onions for storage through the winter At transplanting time you should separate the individual plants the same way as the others, gently tweaking them apart. Onions, by the way, can also be grown from "sets" which are marble-sized miniature onions that go directly into the ground. However, not only do onions started from seed appear to grow larger and cleaner, but they also offer many more varieties to choose from.

- As the onions and leeks grow tall, and start leaning over, you can give them an occasional "haircut" by cutting them back to 3 or 4 inches high.

- Since they go directly from their common pot into the ground, onions and leeks should not be transplanted in direct sunlight. As with all bare-root plants, it must be done in overcast or rainy weather, or in the evening. Water gently.

By early March, you should have your onions, leeks, and marigolds well underway, and endive and several varieties of lettuce in various stages of growing and germinating in their little cups. In the coming weeks, more and more varieties of plants will be sprouting, and the incubator will be rapidly filling up. The next step for them will be the cold frame, covered in chapter 13, but you should first familiarize yourself with the planting schedule in the next chapter to know where you are and where you're going.

Above: Inside view of the incubator on the left, and outside view in the second floor window.

Incidentally…

The tomato was first found by the Spanish conquistadors to be growing in pre-Colombian civilizations in South America. After conquering the native populations, they brought the tomato back to Spain from where it spread worldwide so that today it is probably the most popular vegetable in any home garden.

As I walk around my neighborhood, I find it interesting to see the many and varied places that people grow them. One party will set up a crude, temporary fence around a 3-by-6-foot patch of ground by the side of the house, and put in a few plants. Another party will stick half-a-dozen tiny seedlings in the little strip of dirt, no more than 8 inches wide, that runs between the driveway and the vinyl fence. And still another will place a few plants alongside the chain link fence that separates his front yard from his neighbor's. I see one homeowner growing some plants in an exposed area behind the house, by a back road, where there is very little sun, and where anyone who happens to walk by can pick them.

None of these people expect to break any records, I'm sure, but they are no doubt very happy to be able to put some homegrown tomatoes on the table.

12. Planting Schedule

The Earth is divided into different climate zones ranging from the Arctic to the Tropic, with many variations between the two. Here in the U. S. there are eight zones that irregularly loop their way across the country from north to south. In each zone, winter temperatures differ and spring weather arrives at different times, which means that planting schedules will vary from one zone to another. The following schedule was designed for the Long Island region of New York, which resides in climate zone 7. To utilize this schedule, those living in a different zone will have to revise it upward or downward accordingly. Someone living in the colder zone-six, for example, might want to start 3 weeks later, and those in the warmer zone-eight, 3 weeks earlier, and so on. Check with a local authority to find out your climate zone.

(Although not all the vegetables listed in this schedule will show up in our model garden, they were included here for informational purposes in case you want to try them. All seeds are started in small plastic cups—yogurt, margarine, butter—unless otherwise noted.)

Feb. 7.   Start onions and leeks in 8-to-10-inch tall, wide-mouth containers.

Feb. 21.   Start dwarf marigolds, lettuce and curly endive.

Mar. 5.   Start beets in cups and Sugar Snap peas directly in cell packs, 2 peas per cell. (Beet seeds are compound seeds; two or more seedlings can emerge from each seedpod. Not all pea seeds will take; reseed those cells that do not sprout.)

Mar. 14.   Start more lettuce indoors and some lettuce in the cold frame in a 6-inch-wide plant pot filled with ordinary garden soil. These seeds will remain in the cold frame night and day, and they will take a long time to sprout, but they will be there for you later to fill in empty spaces in the garden. Once they have formed third and fourth sets of leaves, they can go directly into the ground, bypassing the cell stage. Start radish seeds under a tent and peppers, broccoli, broccoli raab, cabbage, and Swiss chard indoors.

Mar. 21.   Onions, leeks, and peas can go in the cold frame, taking them inside at night. One week later, you can leave them in the cold frame day and night, and slowly expose them to the night air.

Apr. 1.   Start tomatoes, cucumbers, and eggplants indoors. Some lettuce can go into the cold frame, daytime only, and a few days later you can put some of these into the ground, under a tent. (More about this in chapter 14.) Onions, leeks, and peas can go into the ground. If the nights are still in the thirties, or the weatherman is predicting some nasty weather ahead, you can wait another week.

Apr. 7. Try a few lettuces in the ground without a tent. If they fare well, as weather moderates more can go in. Meanwhile, keep the tent closed at night and on sunless days, and open it entirely on sunny days, closing it again at night.

Apr. 15. Start basil indoors, and start moving those plants crowding up the incubator into the cold frame. Move a couple chard, raab, and broccoli plants from their cells into 4-inch pots, using garden soil, and hold them in reserve in case any of their cellmates, which will go in the ground in 2 weeks, falter. Things happen, and it's best to be prepared.

Apr. 21. All cool-weather things should be in the cold frame. By now, you can stop taking the plants in at night, both indoors and out, and even leave the cover off the cold frame on pleasant nights in order to acclimate the plants fully to the outdoors.

May 1. All cool-weather things can go into the ground and warm-weathers into the cold frame. Pour a cupful of insecticide into the planting holes of the broccoli and raab and cabbage. For the first week at least, guard the ground plants against unexpected weather. (More about protecting plants in chapter 14.) Plant your bush beans in the ground, two seeds in each hole 6 inches apart, and rows 6 inches apart. Don't make the bean plots so wide that you won't be able to reach inside to pick them. Two feet wide for a medium-height person would be about right. Keep the plot moist until the beans sprout. Thinly scattered grass clippings on the plot will help retain the moisture. If you want to give them a head start, cover the ground with a clear plastic sheet to conserve heat until the beans sprout.

May 7. Look for leaf miner eggs on the undersides of beets and chard, and prepare to spray 5 days after spotting them (see Chapter 21). Spray again 14 days later, and keep monitoring.

May 15. Everything goes in the ground. Start some new broccoli and raab seeds in 4-inch pots outdoors to again serve as emergency backups. Sometimes plants simply quit on you unexpectedly. After sprouting, pinch off all but one of the seedlings so that you will have only one in each pot. Throw the old plants that had been sitting in reserve and have now outgrown their pots into the compost pile.

July 1. Start new broccoli, cabbage, turnips, or raab for a fall crop the same way as those of May15. In the spirit of keeping the garden constantly active and productive, grow a couple extras and hold them in reserve.

July 21. Start some lettuce for a fall crop, first in cups, and then in the cell packs, to be used if and when garden space opens up.

13. INTO THE COLD FRAME

In the middle of March, onions and leeks are growing nicely inside the incubator, you have marigolds, two or three varieties of lettuce, and some curly endive filling two trays of cell packs, and you're running out of room for new plants. This is also the time when some plants are now from 4 to 5 weeks old, and they can benefit greatly by getting out in the fresh air. You are still almost three weeks away from putting anything into the ground so it's cold frame time. Hopefully, you built two of them, and they are in the sunniest place on your patio, preferably up against a wall that will absorb, retain, and reflect back heat. You should line the bottom of the cold frame with Styrofoam, or any other water-shedding material that will insulate the trays from the cold ground. Corrugated plastic, often used as roofing for outdoor structures, could be used.

You should put the seedlings in the cold frame in the morning, and take them inside at night. As in the case of the incubator, allow the sun to heat up the cold frame first. On overcast days, put the top back quickly, and keep the cold frame closed, but when the sun comes out you should open it, more so when the sun is strong, and less so when it's weak. The top should have four cloth-wrapped bricks holding it down at each corner, to keep it from blowing away. (The cloth is used to keep the abrasive bricks from tearing the plastic. Wrap the bricks, and tape them with duct tape.) Open the top by sliding it forward and always keeping the bricks on top to hold it in place. Close monitoring is important. On spring-like days you should remove the cover completely. You want to keep the plants warm, but you don't want to cook them.

By now, most of the plants in the cold frame should be pretty robust, yet still in their little cells, and they could use some extra nourishment. Put some liquid fertilizer in a sprinkling can, and water the plants from the top down, foliage and all. Do this during the day when the leaves still have a chance to dry before nightfall.

Above: Outside view of the cold frames on the left, and inside view on the right.

Incidentally…

One day, a neighbor to whom I had been giving vegetables from my garden for some time, decided that she would like to try growing her own tomatoes and things. "Don't buy any plants," I told her, "I've got some extras that I can give you." And I gave her a few. Several weeks later, when we happened to run into each other, I invited myself into her backyard to see how she was making out. I was taken aback by what I found.

The little patch of ground that she was using, behind the garage, had become completely overshadowed by the trees in her and her other neighbors' yards. The sand-colored ground was hard-packed and covered with weeds. It was very different from when I was last back there, years before, when the former owners had a fairly nice garden growing.

With no preparation of any kind, the neighbor simply punched holes into the hard crust, stuck the plants in, and then dutifully watered them every day. But the plants hadn't grown an inch. In fact, they looked scraggly and yellow, a far cry from how they looked when I turned them over to her.

"Not for nothing," I said, "I don't want to embarrass you in any way, but please come over to my place to see what the possibilities can be."

It was the middle of spring at the time; my garden was fully in place and surging with growth. Some of the cell-pack mates of the plants I gave her were already three feet high and two feet across. Of course, she was stunned. That might have been the day when the idea first reached me that I had a book to write.

14. INTO THE GROUND

Before you do any planting you will have to prepare the ground, and early March is a good time to start filling your containers and leveling the mound of compost. After filling them to the top, line up the containers off to the side so you can move around the garden and break up the top layer of soil with a slight twisting motion with a garden fork. The object is to loosen the soil up without unearthing the leaves that are just below the surface. As the plants send their roots down and out, they will easily work their way through, and thrive on, the decaying leaves. Break up clumps of soil.

Lay out your garden plan by designating with sticks all the spots where your main plants are to go. Drive in your tomato stakes, and then rake the ground smooth. (I use 10-foot metal poles to stake my tomatoes, and I urge new gardeners to start with at least 6-footers. There's more about staking your plants in chapter 16.)

Generally speaking, planting early does not necessarily translate into picking early, and in some cases, it can actually be self-defeating. As mentioned earlier, you mustn't be fooled by the first balmy days that can arrive early in February and March. They can easily get the gardener's blood running, but they are merely teasers. The ground and the nights are still much too cold to support any substantial life. Moreover, there can still be a lot of nasty weather ahead, right through April, so patience will serve you well. Even cool-weather plants will at best merely hang on if planted prematurely, and at worst they will die off completely. In contrast, while early birds are struggling to stay alive in the ground, their cell-pack mates, left in the cold frame, will practically double in size in less than 2 weeks, becoming much sturdier plants. So rather than getting too daring and putting too many things at risk, in most cases it's best to hold back your enthusiasm.

Still, there's something supremely satisfying about picking the first results of all your late-winter activity so there are ways you can try pushing the envelope, ways you can force things by acting selectively and carefully and giving yourself a head start.

Being super hardy, your onions and leeks can go into the ground in the first week of April. Whether they take off quickly or not depends on whether you are having a late or an early spring, but they are tough enough to survive any normal chills that you may get in those early days. Keep your eyes and ears tuned to the weather reports, though. If you see predictions of night temperatures dipping below the forties, it might be a good idea to wait another week.

Peas are perhaps second to onions in their survivability, and they too can be planted at the same time, especially if they had been started indoors in cell-packs and are now 8 to 10 inches high. Like onions, they also may be slow to kick in if spring holds back, but also like onions, once the weather moderates they will surge ahead.

By April 1, the lettuce that was started back in February is growing nicely in their cell-packs and even beginning to overpopulate the incubator. You can start moving them into the cold frame now and even start a test-run in the ground by planting a half-dozen or so. However, April being extremely unpredictable (you can go from spring-like weather to winter-like weather overnight) it's wise to give these early plantings some protection. Cover them with a tent or tunnel made of stiff wire rods bent into U-shapes, stuck into the ground, and covered with clear plastic. Your local home supply center should have wire rods in stock. (An alternative to using rods would be for you to drive 2-foot wooden stakes into the ground on both sides of the plant row, every 18 inches or so, and draping the plastic over them.) Weigh the plastic down with bricks, and open the ends of the tunnel when the sun beats down. Monitor the plants closely because even on cool days the sun's heat can build up to damaging levels inside the tent. Radishes can be started this way as early as late March, and perhaps give you an early salad. See the drawing on the left.

A week later, you can add to the plants under the tent, and try another half-dozen outside the tent, in another part of the garden. In about 2 weeks, the lettuce inside the tent will have grown considerably, despite the continuing cool weather. The others will move more slowly, but when they finally do pick up speed, due to moderating temperatures, it's time to accelerate the plantings and remove the tent.

- Temperatures that unexpectedly dip into the upper thirties in the evenings are not necessarily a death sentence for these cold-hardy crops; they will survive. Still, it's best to move in incremental steps so as not to risk too much, too early.

- Before setting in your plants, run a string or lay a board across the garden to establish a straight line you can follow.

- When planting lettuce and all other row crops, plant them in a triangular pattern; that is, place the second-row plants midway between those of the first row and so on. This will give you maximum spacing between plants.

- Open the tent completely on sunny days, and close it again an hour before the sun weakens. It's the heat stored inside overnight that makes the difference.

- Continue watching the weather reports, and be prepared to shelter any exposed plants with a plastic cover should there be a prediction of an unseasonable snowfall. It can, and often does, happen. Don't lay the plastic directly down on the plants, but use supports to keep the plastic aloft. These unexpected snowfalls are usually followed by typical spring-like days, and the snow disappears quickly so any quick-fix covering will suffice. (I have used my picnic-table benches and stools, draped with plastic sheets, to good effect.) Once the emergency is over and you remove the covers, the plants will be none the worse for wear.

- Plants will slide out of their cell packs more easily if they are allowed to dry out a bit.

Incidentally…

Chapter 21 will discuss a number of destructive insects to be found inside the garden, but let us be preemptive here and first say a few words about some of the beneficial ones. Ladybugs are said to be voracious eaters of aphids. In fact, you can buy them by the package and release them in your garden where you can hope they will stick around to do their thing.

It's hard to label earthworms as insects because they don't do any of the things insects do: bite, sting, fly, or climb, but there they are, in the garden. They spend all their time underground, or in the compost pile, eating organic matter, aerating the soil, and enriching it with their excrement.

We all know, or at least heard, that bees pollinate flowers, and in so doing, perform a great service to mankind. Most fruits are flowers first, and because of the nature of things, those flowers need to be cross-pollinated by other flowers in order to become fruits. (It's a male-female kind of thing.) As the bees, some of them not much larger than mosquitoes, buzz around from flower to flower, looking for nectar, they are inadvertently picking up pollen on their body parts and dropping that pollen off at the next flower. It is all quite unintentional, but it does the job. It is very common in large-scale operations for professional beekeepers to rent out their services by driving their trucks, filled with beehives, from farm to farm, releasing the bees for a spell, and then moving on.

Predatory wasps prey on other insects. They look a lot like those wasps that ruin our picnics, and an untrained eye will never know the difference, but the predatory kinds tirelessly fly around the garden, disappearing for a moment inside a plant or under a leaf, looking for something to eat. Unfortunately, as is the case with the ladybugs and the occasional praying mantis, another predator that will turn up in a garden from time to time, the bad guys overwhelmingly outnumber the good guys so that we can't depend too much on the good guys to control the situation.

15. PICKING AND PLANTING

By the end of April, much of your lettuce should be in place and, believe it or not, the first round almost ready for picking, two weeks before your neighbors will have even begun making their first trips to the garden center to pick up their seedlings. Your onions should be standing 6 inches tall, and the peas should be starting their climb up the trellis. The first lettuce picked should be those growing around the places that had been designated for the long-term plants because those will be soon going in themselves.

All of your cool-weather plants should have been in the cold frames by now, hardening off. More lettuce plants should be ready to be moved out of the cold frame and into those parts of the garden that still have not been planted, waiting for the sun to rise higher.

On May 1 all of your cool-weather plants can go in the ground. Since you grew more seedlings than you are using, you can replant the extras in 4-inch pots and keep them on the side. They will serve as backup plants if any of those in the ground fail for some reason. You can put your bean seeds in the ground, watering them and then covering them with a thin layer of grass clippings left over from last year, to help keep the moisture in. Meanwhile, the tomatoes, peppers, and other warm-weather plants will have been rapidly out-growing the confines of the incubator and should have been gradually shifted into the cold frames, preparing them for final planting in the coming 2 weeks. On May 15 they can go in, and phase one of your planting should be completed, while the picking is just beginning. (Refer again to chapter 12 for the continuing steps in the planting schedule.)

- Although the danger of frost is fairly slim by mid-May, the nights can still be cool and you might want to at least give the tomatoes, the jewels of the garden, some warmth by covering them at sundown with any wide-mouth pots you have available—clay or plastic. Place bricks atop the pots for weight and remember to remove them before the sun comes up.

16. STAKING AND TYING

Tomato plants should be staked. They can grow pretty tall, and they will need the support of a stout pole to keep them off the ground. Most other plants can benefit from staking, too. A broccoli plant, for instance, can get very bulky as it spreads up and out, especially when the main head starts to bulge. A 4-foot stake, driven into the ground alongside the plant shortly after planting time will help the plant to hold that head up later on. Pepper plants, especially bell peppers, can get very top heavy as their fruits pile up, and they will need some assistance. Not only must the main trunks of these plants be supported, but the side branches must as well for they can become so loaded with fruit that they can easily snap under the weight. To prevent that from happening, a tie should be placed around the fruit cluster stem for maximum support. With tomatoes, where as many as 4 or 5 large fruits can form in one bunch, you should do the same thing to keep the stem from tearing away from the branch.

Because plants branch off in many directions, each of the branches becoming heavy with fruit, more than one stake will often be needed. A single pepper plant can easily spread out 36 inches across, and out of the reach of a centrally located stake. You may need to add 3, and even 4, stakes around the plant as it spreads out. Stakes can be purchased at the garden center, but you can make much better ones with the iron rebars that are used to reinforce concrete. These can be bought in home supply centers, will last a lifetime, and can be cut to size with a hacksaw and driven into the ground hard and deep.

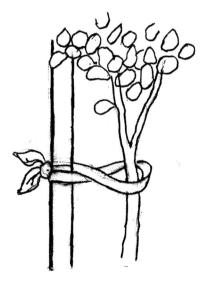

To tie the plants to the stakes, use torn strips of fabric; an old bed sheet is perfect. Loop the strip around the plant stem and twice around the stake before knotting the ends together. As the plant grows, continue tying. See the drawing.

17. Watering Your Plants

The best gift you can give your plants is rainwater. Anyone who has a lawn knows that one good rainfall can accomplish more for a drought-stricken lawn than hours and hours under the sprinkler. The same is true for your garden. Rainwater can perk up a garden like nothing else can, and so it behooves you to do what you can to supply as much of it as you can. (Notice how your garden brightens up after a summer rainstorm.) You can't make it rain, but you can collect it when it does. Place a 33-gallon plastic trash container under one of your home's downspouts, and watch it fill up. Drill a couple holes through the very top of the container, large enough for lengths of 3/8-inch plastic tubing to fit snugly through. Drill a pair of matching holes in a second container, connect the two together with the tubing, and then watch the two containers fill up. Keep several large buckets alongside, to be filled up with spillover, and you can sprinkle your growing menagerie with the elixir of life for as long as the collected water lasts or it continues to rain.

Fully-grown plants in containers will need more watering than those in the ground, especially when the weather is hot and dry. A quart-or-two of water every day should be about right. You'll know it's enough when the water seeps out of the drain holes.

As for the rest of the garden, when to water and how much to water is a judgment call depending again primarily on what the weather has been like, but you must avoid over-watering. When watering with a garden hose, direct the water into the ground, and avoid wetting the foliage, especially in the evening when it won't have enough time to dry. Wet foliage too often will invite disease.

Unfortunately, standing water invites mosquito action so if you notice tiny mosquito larvae swimming around inside the "rain barrels" and buckets, dribble 4 or 5 drops of insecticide lightly on the water so that it floats on the surface. (This will not affect your plants in any way.) The larvae swim to the top to breathe and they will die when they contact the chemical. Repeat as necessary.

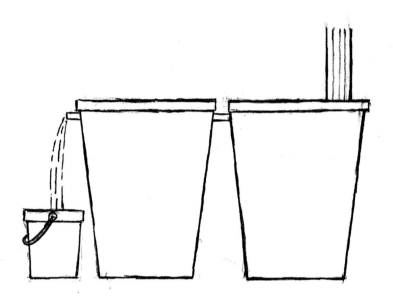

Left: Rainwater collection system. Keep several buckets lined up nearby. When you get a sudden summer storm, dash out and fill them up by dipping the buckets inside the barrels. It will make you feel like a kid again, smelling that smell and playing in the summer rain.

- In time the weight of the water will cause the trash containers to stretch and spring hairline leaks. When that happens you can line the insides of the containers with heavy-duty leaf bags to contain the leaks. This, of course, is easiest done when the containers are empty. Cut snug-fitting holes in the liners for the tubing to squeeze through.

- A great watering tool can be made out of plastic gallon containers. Cut a wide opening around the mouth of the container, and use the handle to scoop out the water.

- At the end of the season, and before the water in the barrels freezes over, use it to wet down the compost pile and the buried leaves. Waste not a drop of it. Turn the containers over for the winter, and weigh them down with bricks.

- When you start your seedlings in February it is too cold to set up the collection system, but you can still arrange to collect a gallon or two of rainwater or melted snow. It is much better than tap water for the emerging plants.

18. FERTILIZING

Once you have your soil to where you want it, rich and fertile, there's little need to add additional fertilizers, except in some situations. Plants growing in buckets or containers will slowly "eat up" the nutrients in the containers. This is clearly evident when you notice that the soil level in the containers is slowly dropping as the season progresses. It becomes even more evident when at the end of the season you dump out the containers and find little more than big, solid root balls. Most of the soil and leaf mold that filled the containers at planting time will have been absorbed and converted into plant material and fruit.

Throughout the season, and while the plants are producing, those nutrients need to be replaced, and a small handful of 5–10–5 fertilizers thrown into the containers every 3 to 4 weeks will do the job.

When planting a second crop it's a good idea to scratch some fertilizer into the soil or into the planting hole to give the plants a head start. Midway through the season, an occasional handful scattered around the larger plants will give them a boost, but keep in mind that excessive fertilizing can cause a plant to grow all foliage and no fruit.

Incidentally…

When I was a boy growing up in Queens County, New York City was far different than it is today, but of course that can be said about every city, town or hamlet everywhere. Queens was an outer-borough, less citified than some of the other boroughs, less developed and populated. There was still a lot of open land there. Many of the people in my town were European immigrants who came from agrarian lands, and they brought with them the farming and gardening culture they grew up with. And so, as far as I can remember, almost everybody had a backyard garden.

I know that my folks did. But the man who lived around the corner from us had much more than a backyard garden. He had two full-sized lots, one on each side of the house that made him a big-time gardener. Perhaps he should be remembered as a small farmer. He grew so much stuff that he sold it, and people came from far around to buy it.

Here was a man who couldn't be luckier. He lived directly across the street from a livery stable. In those days, dirt from excavation sites was hauled away not by truck, but by horse and wagon, and since the horses were boarded here at the stable, they came and went all day long, leaving behind trails of manure. No sooner did the manure hit the ground, this fellow was there with a bucket to scoop it up and take it to his garden. We kids laughed at him, but of course he was giving his plants the best fertilizer known to man.

---

19. Weeding And Mulching

Leave any piece of ground unattended for a few weeks, and that ground will become filled with weeds. The same thing will happen to your garden if attention isn't paid. Weeds come from nowhere and everywhere, and they compete with your plants for nourishment so whenever you spot one, you should pull it out. The easiest way to keep weeds under control, though, is to stop them before they start.

Mulch is a protective material that covers and shades the ground and discourages weed seeds from germinating in the first place. In addition to that, mulch slows down soil evaporation and assists the soil in maintaining even temperatures. Grass clippings, uncontaminated by chemical weed killers, make the perfect mulch in that they can do all that and more. High in nitrogen, they break down slowly and feed the soil. Spread around your plants 2 to 3 inches deep, including inside the containers, and replenished throughout the season, the clippings will never stop working for you. It's wise to set aside a small corner of the yard where you can pile up your grass clippings as you mow your lawn and in this way have a steady supply of them. For several days the fresh clippings, stored in a pile, will heat up considerably due to bacterial action, and will send out a pretty strong odor, but the odor will dissipate soon enough.

Incidentally…

The one thing that is indisputable about Charles Darwin's theory is that only the fittest shall survive. Walk or drive by a piece of unattended land in the peak of the summer heat, by a railroad track, let us say, or an empty lot, and you will see a veritable jungle, a tangle of greenery reaching ten and fifteen feet high, so dense that you couldn't penetrate it even if you wanted to. Weeds, that's what they are, all manner of them, all competing with each other, and all doing very well despite it all. Even if it hasn't rained for a month, and the surrounding landscape and lawns are scorched, the weeds will look green, strong, and standing tall. Throughout the world's history of climate changes, fire, drought, and pestilence, these are the plants that survived unaided.

The interesting thing about them is that as some people say, a weed is anything that you don't want growing in your garden, whatever it is. Queen Anne's lace is a weed that grows wild wherever weeds grow. Granted, the plant itself is not very attractive, but because it's a weed, no one ever takes the time to study its flower closely enough to find that in fact, it's a beautiful thing that looks just like, well, lace. Purple loosestrife is another example of something that you wouldn't want in your garden, and yet it's beauty cannot be denied. They often grow alongside parkways, and the sea of purple they display can only be called stunning.

---

20. PRUNING

A funny thing happens when you cut a branch off a growing plant; in its place will grow two branches. The same thing will happen even if a branch is accidentally broken; at the node closest to the break, two buds will appear and then two branches. This can be either a good thing or a bad thing. If you want to push a plant into growing bushier—an herb for example—you can "pinch off" emerging buds with your thumb and forefinger and thus force the plant to grow more and more branches. It's a bad thing, though, when your reason for the cut was to shrink the plant back because in the end, you will have had the opposite effect of what you intended: more branches than you started off with.

There is one school that encourages the pruning of tomato plants, and another that discourages the practice; it's a coin toss. On the one hand, you certainly will want to remove a branch that's in the wrong place at the wrong time, but on the other hand, pruning away too many branches can lead to a plant going wild with new growth. Those branches that grow out of the base of a tomato plant and meander several feet in length without flowering should certainly be pruned out. These are commonly referred to as suckers, and they serve no function. And yes, a branch that's vigorously growing in the wrong place and in the wrong direction, making your efforts to keep the plant contained, should be removed, but beyond that you should proceed carefully because for almost every branch you eliminate, two will take its place.

In the case of an herb plant that has been picked heavily all season long, and has come to look a bit tired and scraggly, it can be cut back to its lower tiers and experience an almost complete resurgence so pruning definitely has some clear benefits. When pruning, always cut at the point where you want the new growth to form—just above a joint or node facing outward. The bottom line when it comes to pruning is to be judicious.

- Cut away the flower stalks that grow out of basil and onion plants. They are in the process of forming seeds, and that pulls energy out of the plants.

21. Looking For Trouble

The banes of the gardener's existence are insects. Insects come in many varieties, and they all have one thing in common: they are here to make our lives miserable. Well, that's only partly true. Actually, they are here to perpetuate the species, and they do that by eating (voraciously) mating (all the time) and reproducing (incredibly). They say that there are more varieties of insects in the world than any other species of living things, and judging by the numbers in our gardens that's easy to believe.

Different insects have different preferences in their choices of food. Some like this, and some like that. Aphids, one of the most common pests in the garden, are an exception. They will attach themselves to practically anything you grow, sucking the juices from a plant, introducing diseases, and eventually bringing the plant to an early demise. Fortunately, though, it turns out that aphids, ubiquitous though they may be, are one of the easiest insects to control by simply setting out a bunch of potted marigold plants around the garden. It looks like aphids can't stand marigolds, and no sooner do they arrive when the marigolds send them packing. For a small garden, eight or ten plants spread around will do the job.

Most other pests, however, are more specialized than aphids in their choices of habitat: tomato hornworms, for instance. They are fat, green, caterpillar-like creatures, the thickness of your little finger at full maturity, and they will usually be found only on your tomato plants. They can work their way through a plant, stripping bare whole leaves, and even chewing out half a green tomato before you notice their existence. Even if you do spot one and remove it, you have to assume that many others, in different stages of growth, are lurking around. They have the perfect camouflage, being the exact color of tomato leaves, which makes them extremely difficult to find even after you discover the tell tale signs of their existence—clumps of excrement, stripped leaves, tomatoes partly eaten. If you spray the plant with insecticide you will find their carcasses littering the ground the next day. Very often, that one spray will do it for the season, but you can repeat it if and when you need to.

Leaf miners like plants of the spinach, Swiss chard and beet varieties. The leaf miner bugs start life as a series of tiny fly-deposited white eggs lined up very precisely in rows on the undersides of leaves. The eggs hatch into equally tiny grubs that penetrate the leaves and tunnel their ways between the top and bottom tissues, leaving discolored blotches behind that grow in size as the grubs eat their way through. If you hold one of these leaves up to the light, you can see the grubs in shadow, wiggling around inside. Spray the tops and bottoms of the leaves 4 to 5 days after you first spot the eggs, and again 14 days later. After the first treatment, continue to look for the telltale blotches that indicate that the grubs are on the move again, and spray when you see them.

Root maggots also start out as eggs, deposited in the soil at the bases of the broccolis, cabbages, and other members of the crucifer family of vegetables. The adult flies of the species lay their eggs, and the maggots that hatch feed on the roots of the plants unnoticed at first until one day when a plant that looked perfectly healthy the night before suddenly appears wilted. A deep watering seems to help it recover, but the next day it's wilted again, and beyond help. When you pull the plant out of the ground you will find atrophied roots, infested with maggots. Purists may prefer to control these pests by placing a flat collar made from tarpaper, carpeting, or other pliant material around the stem of the plant at planting time to keep the fly from crawling down the stem and laying its eggs, but the flies don't need much of an opening to slip past the collar and do their work so the collar treatment is not as effective as pouring a cupful of insecticide down the planting hole.

Another nemesis of the crucifers is the cabbage moth, the chalky white "butterfly" that we used to chase and capture when we were kids. They lay their eggs on the undersides of leaves, and the tiny green worms that emerge eat away with such determination that the leaves could easily begin to look like Swiss cheese if left unattended. Spraying the bottoms of the leaves is in order here too.

Even within the same species of plants, there are examples of insects preferring one variety above others, and no better example can be given than that of the pepper maggots, which also start out as fly-eggs. In the same garden, bell peppers can be plagued with maggots while their cousins, sweet or hot, will go unscathed. For this reason, bell peppers will require spraying while the others may not. For all situations, get yourself a pump sprayer, read the insecticide labels to see if they control those insects you are after, and follow the directions carefully.

Very often, you may find a small plant lying on the ground in the morning, looking as though someone had cut it off with a scissor right at the soil line. Oddly, if you replace the plant, chances are that the very next morning the new plant will have suffered the same fate. This is a sign of the existence of a cutworm that comes out at night and eats through the stem of the plant. The usual recommendation made to control cutworms is for the gardener to encircle a cylindrical paper collar around newly planted seedlings to keep the cutworms from reaching the stems, but because of the number of plants you will be dealing with, that strikes me as impractical. Cutworms are some of the least problematic bugs in terms of their numbers, and the fact that they usually return to the same spot for their next-night's meal suggests that they don't wander much so if you sprinkle some powdered insecticide at the base of the replacement plant, you will probably find one very dead cutworm lying there the next morning, never to bother you again.

- The reason for growing marigolds in pots are twofold: They can be moved around the garden as needed and, if planted directly into the garden, even dwarf marigolds can aggressively take over too much space.

- Insects wouldn't be here on Earth in so many numbers if they didn't have a trick or two up their sleeves and know how to fight back. If they find the plant of their choice too inhospitable, they are not squeamish about breaking pattern and seeking out a different host to feed on so you've got to keep your eyes open at all times. If a plant looks damaged, inspect it closely.

- Try always to spray in the late evening, at dusk, when bee activity has ended. Bees pollinate our plants, and we don't want to be killing them off, too.

- Don't be turned off by the thought of spraying insecticides on your plants. Bell peppers need careful monitoring, as do beets and Swiss chard, but they are exceptions. Some plants require just one or two sprayings in a season, and many none at all. Besides, the chemicals dissipate quickly, and what remains is easily washed off in the kitchen.

Finally, damping off is the term given to the plant disease that affects seedlings inside the incubator in their earliest stages of growth. Just days old, the seedlings simply topple over and die, and when you examine them carefully, you find that their tiny stems have shriveled up at the soil line. This is what can happen when you try starting seeds in ordinary soil, and it's one of the reasons for using sterilized seeding mixture. By the time the seedlings are ready to be moved into cell packs, they've become less sensitive to impurities, and you can safely transplant them into the soil you saved for the purpose.

Incidentally…

One can live with the idea of growing a garden without chemical fertilizers, especially when the soil is fertile, but growing a garden using no insecticides is another story. I tried it in my early days and found that it didn't work; at least not for me. Can you look for tomato hornworms and pick them off with a gloved hand, one by one, as some recommend? Yes, and I've done that, but as already stated, being the exact color of the plants themselves, they are extremely tough to find, and it's doubtful that you can ever find them all.

When you spot the insect eggs on the bottoms of your beet leaves, can you wash them off? Yes again, and I've done that, too, but only while the plants are few and small. As they grow in size and number, turning into a crowd, it gets much tougher to look under every leaf. Of course, you can do what others suggest, and try growing beets under a screen or netting, to keep the egg-laying flies away, but how practical is that when you've got to water, weed, mulch, and constantly attend to them? Swiss chard, much larger plants than beets, fall prey to the same flies. Can you throw a net around them? And how about all the other plants in the garden, all of whose insect problems start with flies? Can you cover them all? Certainly not, no more than you can go around the garden picking off every bug, beetle, or worm that lies therein.

Pest management is the answer. Know the enemy, its habits and its patterns, spray it at the right time(s), and you'll win the battle. The more you practice it, the easier it becomes.

Above: Photo shows a potted marigold in the foreground, a staked tomato plant to its right, some onions running alongside the raised bed wall, three varieties of lettuce, and Swiss chard in the background. Marigolds like this one, spread around the garden, keep aphids away. As the lettuce is picked, the other plants will fill the open spaces.

Incidentally…

I convinced my neighbor, whose backyard was overwhelmed by trees, that container gardening was going to be her only option if she had any hopes of growing anything. There were a couple of spots back there where some breaks in the trees, and shifting sun, allowed some sunlight to squeeze through at different times of the day. I added that she might have to move the containers around a bit, chasing the sun, if she wanted to maximize her results, but that would be up to her.

A few days later she invited me in to see her setup. Instead of the at least 5-gallon buckets I had recommended, she had bought some wide flowerpots, about a foot deep, and she filled them halfway with potting soil. Inside were some grape tomato seedlings.

It was still not my wish to criticize or embarrass her so, although I suggested that I would have done it differently, I wished her luck, and promised her that she would at least have fun with it. And she did. Some time later, my bell rang, and there she was at the door with a handful of little tomatoes, happily offering me some of her very first pick of the crop.

22. ANIMAL CONTROL

Some gardeners have to put up with deer, and some with rabbits or both, but if your area is anything like mine, squirrels are your most common pests. To them a garden is a combination sand box and food pantry. They love to dig holes in the soil everywhere, seemingly at random, but what they are probably really doing is digging around for food caches that they buried some time before. You realize this when at the end of the season you are going through the soil rebuilding process, and you are turning up dozens of apples that had mysteriously disappeared from your apple tree throughout the summer, and peanuts that first puzzled you but puzzle you no more.

It's more than annoying to step out one morning and find that something has dug a hole, and in the process has torn up several small plants in close proximity to that hole. Or worse, something has dug several holes in the patch where you had just planted your beans. This will go on all season long if you can't find a way to stop it. Mothballs don't help, blood meal doesn't help, and even relocating the squirrels—often illegal, by the way—doesn't seem to help. Members of another tribe soon fill the voids that are left behind.

Here is one method, left, that works. After you've put in your major plants—the tomatoes, peppers, etc.—circle them with 4–5 bricks. This will create a barrier around the plants that will block the squirrels. They seem to show no inclination to climb over the bricks and dig around the plant.

Where you've got lettuce or other row crops growing, and you can't surround each plant with bricks, you can fill the spaces between the rows with sticks, boards, some bricks—anything that will make it difficult for the squirrels to get in there to dig. (The slats from an old stockade fence are perfect for this.) This has the effect of turning the garden into an obstacle course that the squirrels seem reluctant to deal with. In the cases where you plant seeds directly in the ground—beans, peas—you can lay out the slats first, and then plant the seeds between them. Weighing the slats down randomly with bricks and rebars to keep them in place makes it all the more daunting for the squirrels to intrude.

Above: Assortment of wooden slats, iron rebars, aluminum sticks, and bricks discourage squirrels from poking around while young plants are given a chance to grow.

- Neighborhood cats often see a garden as a giant litter box, and these measures also work to keep them in check.

- Once the garden is fully developed and dense, the squirrels will show no tendency to penetrate the maze of plants, always preferring open ground, At that point you can either remove the slats and other obstructions, or leave them there for the rest of the season. They create no problems.

Incidentally…

Some might think that there could not be much of a difference between the temperatures inside and outside a plastic-enclosed tunnel, but consider how hot it gets inside a car that's been sitting in the sun for a while. In fact, on a clear sunny day, even with the ends of a tunnel open, you can find that some of the plants inside may wilt because of the pocket of hot air trapped in the middle, unable to escape. That's when a tunnel needs to be opened completely.

These differences, of course, also exist around the cold frame. By closing it up at night, just before the last of the sun's rays strike it, you can warm up the interior before temperatures fall. Protected further from the chill winds outside, during that tentative time before those night temperatures finally climb into the fifties, plants inside the cold frame will outpace those in the ground. On the other hand, since the ground plants have more room in which to spread their roots, the best-case scenario is to have the plants in the ground and under a tent.

23. Planting A Second Crop

Because we want our garden to always be in full production, with little dead time in between picking, it is important to remind ourselves about succession planting. As mentioned earlier, beets, beans, peas, and broccoli, to name just a few, can be grown twice in one season, in some instances because they are fast growers and get picked whole, and in other instances because after having been picked over for a length of time, they've become pretty exhausted, and it's time to pull them out and make room for more.

The broccoli plant is a large plant that grows into a main head that when sliced off with a sharp knife will make way for a succession of smaller heads, or clusters. Over time the clusters will keep getting smaller until they are no longer worth picking, and it becomes time to retire the plant, but you should be prepared for this because on July 15 you should have started some new seeds that should now be ready to take over for the spent plants.

Broccoli raab, that hugely popular vegetable favored in Italian restaurants, forms small flower clusters that are picked just before the flowers open up. Their clusters also get fewer and smaller until the plant can be replaced with seedlings begun at the same time as the second-generation broccoli.

Beans and peas, after giving you 4–5 pickings over a couple weeks time, will drop off suddenly and allow you time for a second sowing in the same spots. Beets, which had been planted in stages so as to give you a regular flow of them, can be replaced as they are picked, using the new seedlings that have been growing in cell packs. All of this is detailed in the planting schedule chapter.

- Seedlings are much easier to grow indoors in the winter and outdoors in the spring than they are when the sun gets hot. In summertime it's best to keep them in filtered sun, in the partial shade of a tree, perhaps.

Incidentally…

A friend bought an old chicken farm for a weekend retreat, and he kept a few animals around. My then-teenage daughter joined me one day to visit him. I couldn't resist putting some manure in the hatchback. The aroma was, well, interesting. I reveled in the idea of it; my daughter made faces. Still, we laughed ourselves silly all the way home.

---

24. Keeping A Diary

You'll have a lot of hits and misses as you go along, and the best way to learn from both is to keep a diary. At the end of every season, make a note of everything that went right and everything that went wrong, and the reasons why you think they happened. The following season, refresh yourself with what you wrote, and see if you can't repeat the good results and avoid the bad. If unsure about something, talk to someone at your neighborhood garden nursery, or call your local cooperative extension. Even if and when things turn out less than you had hoped for, you will have had a lot of fun. As the successes multiply, so will the fun.

Above: Photo shows three picked heads of Romaine lettuce next to a three-foot yardstick. This is a success story.

25. Summation

This chapter will attempt to bring the season into focus by reviewing everything we've learned so far, plus a few things more. Many of the statements you find here may seem redundant, but they are important enough to bear repeating and keep remembering. The things that cannot be repeated often enough are that you can't grow everything, and you can't eat everything so you shouldn't aim too high, at least in the beginning. It's far better to have fewer but stronger plants than to have more but weaker ones. In the end, the fewer will be far more productive than the many. Once you get more experienced you can get more experimental.

When putting the very first plants into the ground in early April, it's too easy to get carried away and overplant. There'll be so much room to work with in the beginning it will be tempting to bunch them up, but once things get going it will take very little time for those tiny plants to become big plants and then very big plants. One lettuce plant, for example, when fully-grown, can easily spread a foot across, as the photo in the preceding chapter shows. So can endive. Other major plants can grow to 3 feet wide. A general rule of thumb, therefore, is to separate all your main plants by at least 2 ½ feet.

Here, in the rough order of their appearance in the garden, are some final tips that will hopefully make your gardening experience a fruitful one.

Onions: Growing so tightly in a small pot, their roots will be tangled. When transplanting, tease apart the roots carefully on a rainy day or in the evening. They are tough and will survive some root breakage. If the root ball is allowed to dry out a bit for a day or so, it will come apart more easily. Poke holes in the ground with your finger, and stick the plants in 4 to 6 inches apart in rows 6 inches apart. When pencil thick, mulch them with grass clippings. They are ready to be picked when the foliage falls over and starts to turn yellow. After pulling them out, tie them in bunches and hang them outside in a shady spot to dry. Take them inside when it turns cold.

Leeks: They look very much like onions in their early stages. Grow them in a trench 12 inches deep and 6 inches wide. Line the bottom of the trench with 3 inches of compost. In this 6-inch-wide trench you can grow two rows of leeks, alternately spaced 3–4 inches apart. Gradually fill the trench with soil and compost. When mature, pull them out by grabbing the stalks by their very bottoms and pulling hard.

Sugar Snap Peas: Not all seeds will "take". Place two seeds in each cell, and reseed where they fail to sprout. Go for the string-less, bush type. Peas can be grown up a trellis or net as many as 5 or 6 plants in a 5-gallon container, or in the ground, 2 inches apart in rows at least 2 ½ inches apart. They have a relatively short life, and in their place you can follow up with bush beans, turnips, or more peas later in the season. Peas are intolerant of hot weather.

Marigolds: They tend to bud and flower earlier in the constraints of their cell packs than they do in larger spaces so it's a good idea to move them into 10-to-12-inch pots after the first flowers form, not before. By starting them early they will be ready for lettuce-planting time when the aphids first make their appearance.

Lettuce: Plant them 8 inches apart wherever your main crop plants will be going in later. As they spread into each other, pull them alternately to make room for them to grow bigger.

Beets: Space them 6 inches apart, in rows 6 inches apart. Try to keep a steady supply of them by starting new seedlings every 3 weeks or so to replace those being pulled. In hot weather, keep the seedlings in filtered sun. Beets are magnets for the leaf miner, so stay on top of them. Mulch heavily to control weeds. Pull them out when they're 3 to 4 inches across. The leaves, cooked separately, are delicious.

Broccoli: At planting time, pour a cupful of insecticide into the hole. It's a pretty substantial plant that becomes very top heavy. Use a 4-foot stake driven deeply to support it. Holes in the leaves indicate tiny green worm activity on their undersides, and will require spraying. Spray the bottoms of the leaves only. When the plants have petered out they can be replaced with more broccoli, cabbage, or any other cold-weather plant. Broccolis are even better fall plants than spring plants, producing well into the cool weather.

Broccoli Raab: Same as broccoli.

Cabbage: Same as broccoli.

Swiss Chard: It will keep producing well into late fall. Cut out the outer leaves at their bases, and they will be replaced with new ones. They are a leaf miner favorite so monitor them carefully.

Bush Beans: Be reminded that if you have animal problems you can set the seeds down between boards or slats. Mulch heavily once the plants are established. Drive stakes into the four corners of the bed and string twine around the stakes to form a "cage" around the plants to keep them upright as they grow.

Basil: In our planting schedule, the basil is timed to peak at tomato salad time because that's when we like it most. It could certainly be started earlier if you prefer.

Bell Peppers: The plants can grow quite large, and when laden with fruits, the branches can easily break off. Sturdy staking and tying is a must. Give them the room and support they need, and two plants can fill your freezer with stuffed peppers. They lend themselves to container planting, but those in the ground will be much bigger. (This is true for all container-grown plants.) You won't know that a bell has maggots inside until the pepper falls to the ground, and then it's lost. Spraying every 2 weeks may be necessary in some cases, but they're worth it. (First-time gardeners may not see these and the other insects we've discussed, in the first year or two. It sometimes takes time for them to find us, but once they do they never leave.) Incidentally, all peppers turn red if left to grow long enough.

Tomatoes: They are best planted deeply, at least up to the first set of true leaves, or even deeper still. This is especially true if the plants are on the spindly side. Pinch or cut off the leaves that would have been buried below the soil line. Roots will grow out of the underground stem, making it a much stronger plant. A happy tomato plant can easily climb a 10-foot pole and still want more, but you can start more modestly than that, at least until you see how your garden grows. If you should spot a tomato hornworm with what looks to be a lot of rice grains attached to its back, leave it alone. Those are actually parasites in the act of destroying the hornworm, and you can use all the help you can get.

Turnips: We don't show them in our diagrammed model garden or our planting schedule because we don't grow them every year, but rather on a whim. When we do, we grow them in containers where expired beans or peas have been removed. They can be started in cups, then cell packs, the same as all others.

All plants: Remove them from their cell packs by pushing gently from the bottom with your thumb and squeezing the sides when the root balls are semi-dry. Set them into the garden a shade lower than ground level and press in gently, filling in the resulting impression with soil. To avoid plant shock it's best to avoid hot sun.

Incidentally…

Back in the "Good Old Days", in the nineteenth century, when people were more obliged to grow their own food than they are today, home gardening was a twelve-month affair. They used any and all means at their disposal to put food on the table, store it, and preserve it.

To grow food during the cold winter months, they built hothouses in which to grow their plants, and hotbeds in which to start their seedlings. To heat them both, they relied on the heat generated by decomposing organic matter. Inside the hothouses, they would dig deep pits and fill them with as many as 7–8 feet of leaves. As the leaves slowly broke down, they could generate enough heat to warm these glassed-in enclosures for an entire year, allowing for the cultivation of all kinds of plants. In the hotbeds, they would line the bottoms with several feet of stable dung before covering it with a foot of earth, and then setting pots in the earth in which to start their seeds.

Remarkably, the thing these farmers and gardeners had to be constantly on guard against was the buildup of too much heat, requiring them to crack open some of the windows from time to time to release some of the excess heat.

---

26. Wrapping It Up

It's hard to imagine, but by the time you pick the last of your crops, you will have spent the better part of the year, from early February through October, and perhaps even into November, tending your plants and garden, and you will be ready for a break. In the same way you will have had your fill of the summer heat and start to look forward to a change of season, so will it be with the garden. But also, in the same way that the first blast of chill air that arrives from the north has you quickly longing once more for those bright, sunny days just gone by, you will just as suddenly begin to miss the garden.

You will miss sowing your very first seeds, and then anxiously waiting for them to sprout. You will miss watching the incubator slowly fill up with seedlings, bursting with light and energy; waking up in the morning and seeing your bedroom wall ablaze with sunlight, earlier every day, and then hustling the seedlings into the incubator; moving your trays into the cold frame and gradually exposing them to more and more fresh air; setting the plants in the ground; watching them grow; and finally picking their fruits.

Most of all, you will miss the serenity you feel when you are out in the garden on a quiet summer day, contemplating the mysteries of life that cause so many beautiful things to come out of the bare ground.

But meanwhile, there's work to be done. There are pits to be dug, leaves to be buried, compost piles to be started, diaries to be updated, and plans to be made for the following spring. And before you know it, December will melt into the New Year, February will roll around, and it will be time to start all over again.

Happy wintering.

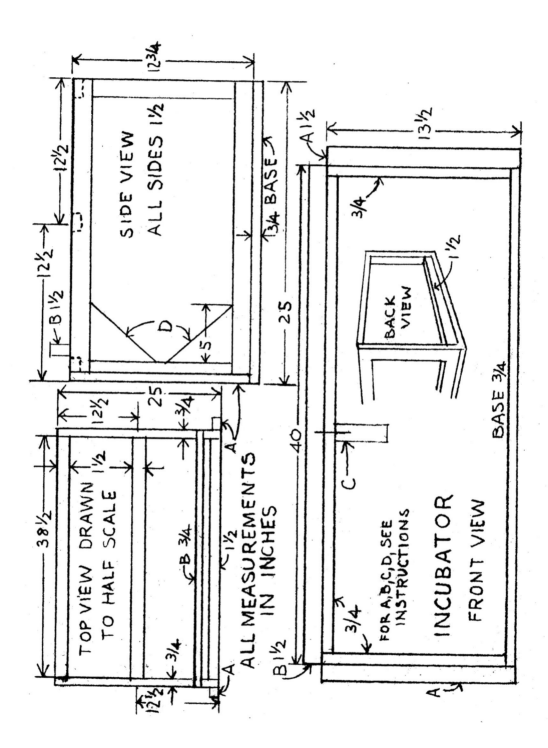

SIDE VIEW
ALL SIDES 1½

12¾

12½

12½

B 1½

¾ BASE

D

5

25

40

B 1½

TOP VIEW DRAWN
TO HALF SCALE

ALL MEASUREMENTS
IN INCHES

38½

12½

25

¾

1½

B ¾

A

1½

A

12½

¾

A 1½

13½

¾

1½

BACK
VIEW

BASE ¾

25

C

¾

FOR A, B, C, D, SEE
INSTRUCTIONS

¾

A

INCUBATOR
FRONT VIEW

27. Construction Diagrams And Instructions

Notes On Building The Incubator:

A: Stop blocks rest against the window frame, keeping the box from falling out.

B: Stop block rests against the window sash, keeping the box from creeping in.

C: Wooden dowel gives you something to hold onto when lifting the box in and out of the window.

D: Braces used for strength, approx. 5 inches on the two right-angle sides.

Except for the base, which is ¾-inch plywood, and the corner braces—letter D in the drawing, cut from 1-by-6-inch board—the incubator box is made from 1-by-2-inch furring strips (actual measurements: ¾-by-1.5-inches). If you can't find perfectly straight furring strips, you or your lumberman can rip them out of a pine board. The measurements shown for the box assume a window opening of 41 inches wide and 16 inches high with the window raised. Your window will probably have different dimensions so you'll have to figure out your own measurements. The box must be 1 inch shorter than your window opening in both width and height to allow for sliding into place. The depth dimensions remain the same. The sides, top, and back of the box are covered with plastic of at least 4 to 6 mils thickness or heavier. Exposed to the wind and sun, the plastic will in time tear and require replacement, and the heavier material will last longer. The room side of the box is always open; it's the heat from the room that moderates the temperature inside the box on sunless days.

The incubator pictured here is identical to the one I've been using for many years except for one difference: Mine is a wooden double-hung window with a storm window attached to the outside window frame, the storm window opening being slightly narrower than the window itself by 2.5 inches on each side. With that arrangement, I was able to use the storm window to hold the box in place, and that allowed me to install the box flush with the storm window which enables me to pull the inside window down at night when the plants are taken in. The configuration shown here assumes that there is no storm window so the stop blocks must rest against the inside window frame instead of the storm window in my case, putting the box into the path of the window sash. This means that during the cold months, the box will have to be taken in at night, a simple enough task since it should slide in and out easily. But if taking the box in and out every night is too much of a hassle, you can block out the night air with cardboard, blankets or any other suitable material. It may not be pretty, but it's only for a couple months.

A storm window installation differs in the following respects: you build the box to fit through the storm window opening, rather than through the inside window opening. Now, in place of the window sash stop block, which is there to prevent the box from drifting in, you need to attach a one-inch-quarter-round molding to the bottom of the incubator base at the point where it sits on the storm window frame. Two sheet metal screws going through the molding and into the storm window frame will keep the box stationary. *Important:* A storm window is usually secured to the outside window frame with just a few screws. If it is to bear the weight of the box it will have to be reinforced with at least a dozen more screws along both sides.

Painting the wood parts with exterior paint will give them protection against the humidity that builds up inside the box. My box was built around a base that came from a discarded Formica-covered sink top so it has a smooth surface for the plant trays to slide on. You can cover your base with a sheet of Plexiglas. Drill a couple weep holes through the base in the back of the box for water runoff to escape.

A word of caution must be posted here: A large window box, the size of mine, is pretty heavy, and when filled with plants, it gets heavier still. In addition, on windy days it will have to withstand some serious buffeting about so it is essential that the box be well built and securely installed. Look again at the photos of my incubator in chapter 11 to imagine the forces at work.

You must first make sure that your window and its frame are strong enough for the task. If the window you are using is on the ground floor, a couple 2 by 4s, used as legs between the ground and the box, will keep it propped up, making for a simpler installation, but an upper level window requires more thought. A heavy wooden double-hung window frame and sash, like mine, are more than adequate to keep the box locked in place, but a lighter-weight aluminum or vinyl window will need some extra help—a wooden 2 by 3, perhaps, running from edge to edge inside the window channel. A skilled hand should be able to figure something out. Just keep in mind that safety trumps everything. Once the box is in place, seal out air leaks with tape, putty, towels, or anything else that will keep cold air out.

Materials needed to construct the incubator:
¾-inch exterior plywood, 40 by 25 inches.
4 eight-footers, 1-by-2-inch furring strips.
Wooden dowel, 1.5 by 5 inches long.
1-by-6-inch board, 1 foot long.
Plastic sheeting, 4–6 mils or higher.

Construction Tips: use exterior glue except when noted, and exterior screws:
Construct the two sides using lap joints and 3/4-inch nails. Flatten the nail points that stick out.
Attach each corner brace to the sides, attached from both the inside and outside, with four 2.5-inch screws.
Attach each side to the base from the bottom up with four 2-inch screws. Countersink them.

Attach the three cross-members at the top with two 2.5-inch screws at each joint. Keep everything flush.

Attach the handgrip from the top down with one 2.75-inch screw.

Cut the bottom rail in the back of the box to size, and attach it to the bottom and sides, using 2-inch screws.

Staple the top, sides and back of the box with double-layered plastic, folding it in ways to direct rainwater away from getting inside the box.

Attach each frame stop from the inside out with four 2-inch screws. Use no glue.

With the box in the window, pull the window sash down and determine its back edge.

Attach the sash stop with three 2-inch screws to fit behind the sash. Use no glue.

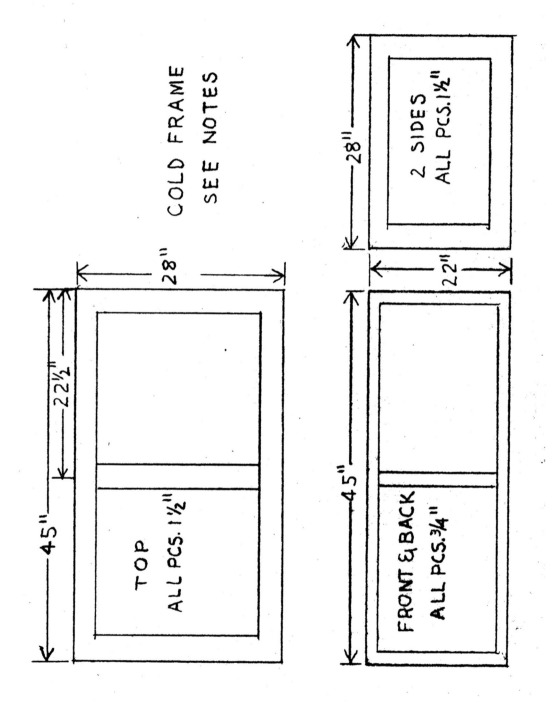

COLD FRAME
SEE NOTES

28"

2 SIDES
ALL PCS. 1½"

28"

22"

22½"

45"

TOP
ALL PCS. 1½"

45"

FRONT & BACK
ALL PCS. ¾"

Notes On Building The Cold Frame:

Materials needed:
Five 8-footers, 1-by-2-inch furring strips.
Eight 2-by-¼-inch stove bolts, sixteen nuts and eight washers.
Tarpaper to fit.
Plastic Sheeting.

The cold frame is built to be taken apart for storage in the winter so the sides, front, back, and top are all separate and attachable. The front and back will be bolted to the sides, and the top is freestanding.

Construction Tips: Use exterior glue throughout.
Construct the five components using the same techniques used in constructing the incubator. Clamp together one of the sides to one end of the front section, making sure both wood strips are mated perfectly. Drill two 1/4-inch holes, evenly spaced and through the middle of both strips. Before unclamping them, mark both pieces with an indelible marker so that these two components can always be matched up when reassembling the box. Do this on all four corners where the sides meet the front and back. Push a 2-by-¼-inch stove bolt through each of the holes in the front and back frames, from the inside out, and thread a nut on the bolt. Before tightening them, remove enough material from the hole so that the nut will recede into the hole and be flush with the wood surface. The bolts will remain in place permanently, and the sides can be slipped on and off using washers and nuts to hold them in place.

For greater longevity, paint the framework. For greater plant protection, all but the back sections of the cold frame will have plastic on both sides. Wrap the plastic around each section and staple it in place in a way to minimize water entry. The trapped air between the two layers will give some insulation. Drill two ¼-inch weep holes through the bottom rails of the four members of the box to allow for escape of any rainwater that does find its way in. Cut away the plastic around the boltholes in the sides and run some staples around the holes to keep the plastic from tearing away. The back section has tarpaper on both sides. The black paper will absorb heat, and the space inside will help retain it. When finished, the box can be assembled and disassembled by slipping the sides over the bolts.

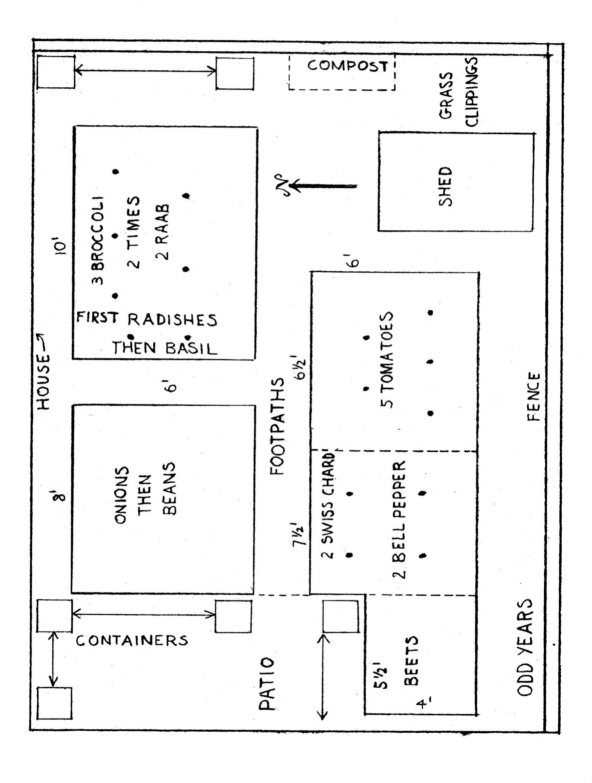

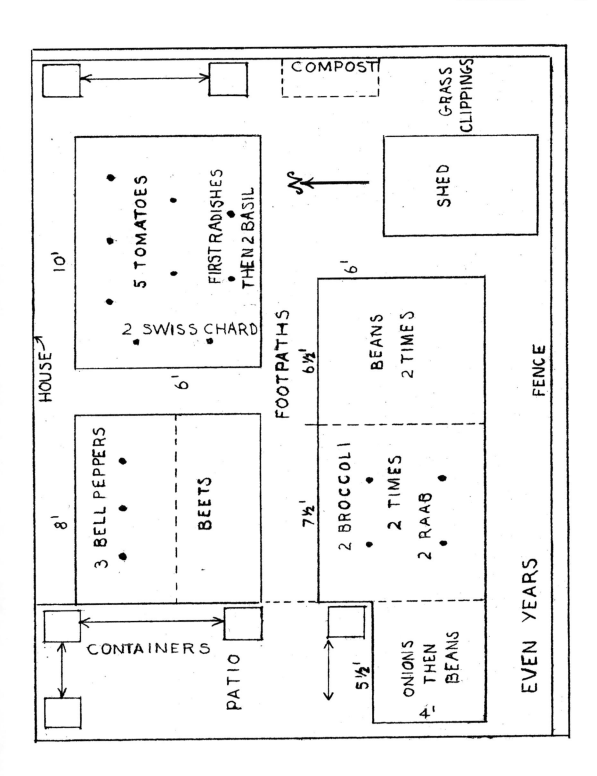

BOOK INDEX

978-0-595-39322-(
0-595-39322-5

Printed in the United States
72418LV00005B/33

9 780595 393220